G000067570

Public Service Accountability

Peter Murphy · Laurence Ferry
Russ Glennon · Kirsten Greenhalgh

Public Service Accountability

Rekindling a Debate

Peter Murphy
Nottingham Business School
Nottingham Trent University
Nottingham, UK

Russ Glennon
Nottingham Business School
Nottingham Trent University
Nottingham, UK

Laurence Ferry
Durham Business School
Durham University
Thornaby, UK

Kirsten Greenhalgh
University of Nottingham Business
School
University of Nottingham
Nottingham, UK

ISBN 978-3-319-93383-2 ISBN 978-3-319-93384-9 (eBook)
https://doi.org/10.1007/978-3-319-93384-9

Library of Congress Control Number: 2018943630

© The Editor(s) (if applicable) and The Author(s) 2019
This work is subject to copyright. All rights are solely and exclusively licensed by the Publisher, whether the whole or part of the material is concerned, specifically the rights of translation, reprinting, reuse of illustrations, recitation, broadcasting, reproduction on microfilms or in any other physical way, and transmission or information storage and retrieval, electronic adaptation, computer software, or by similar or dissimilar methodology now known or hereafter developed.
The use of general descriptive names, registered names, trademarks, service marks, etc. in this publication does not imply, even in the absence of a specific statement, that such names are exempt from the relevant protective laws and regulations and therefore free for general use.
The publisher, the authors, and the editors are safe to assume that the advice and information in this book are believed to be true and accurate at the date of publication. Neither the publisher nor the authors or the editors give a warranty, express or implied, with respect to the material contained herein or for any errors or omissions that may have been made. The publisher remains neutral with regard to jurisdictional claims in published maps and institutional affiliations.

Cover credit: © Melisa Hasan

Printed on acid-free paper

This Palgrave Macmillan imprint is published by the registered company Springer International Publishing AG part of Springer Nature
The registered company address is: Gewerbestrasse 11, 6330 Cham, Switzerland

ACKNOWLEDGEMENTS

We would like to thank our publisher Palgrave and, in particular, Oliver Foster our editorial assistant and Jemima Warren the senior commissioning editor who first took on the project, together with the anonymous reviewers of our original proposal.

The origin of this book is a report that Laurence and Peter produced for the National Audit Office. We would like to thank the NAO who commissioned and (part) funded that report. Any errors or omissions in that work or this are the responsibility of the author(s), and the NAO does not necessarily endorse the findings of the work.

At the other end of the project, we would like to thank Katarzyna Lakoma our Research Assistant at Nottingham Business School, but for her help, we would never have got this done on time!

Finally, and not least we would also like to acknowledge the continuous support, patience, and understanding of our respective families throughout the writing process and more.

Laurence would like to thank his wife Anchalee and daughters Dior and Eloise, and especially his mam Hazel and father Laurence (now deceased) who continually taught him to question, not be afraid to challenge authority and hold people to account.

Russ would like to thank his colleagues at NTU who supported him during the writing of the book, and especially his wife, Jo, and son, Elliot; Jo's proofreading of the manuscript was particularly above and beyond the call of duty.

Kirsten would like to thank husband Rob and their sons Dan and Josh, and Peter would like to thank, as ever Steph and Rob.

CONTENTS

About the Authors

Peter Murphy is Professor of Public Policy and Management and Head of Research at Nottingham Business School, Nottingham Trent University, UK. He is Vice Chair (Research) of the Public Administration Committee of the Joint Universities Council and a member of the Advisory Board of the Centre for Public Scrutiny. Prior to joining academia in 2009, he was a Senior Civil Servant and the Chief Executive of a Local Authority.

Laurence Ferry is Professor of Accounting at Durham University, UK, Parliamentary Academic Fellow 2018/2019 looking at public accountability and Fellow of the Chartered Institute of Public Finance and Accountancy. He is a well-recognised international expert in public financial management having published over 100 outputs and worked with governments across 30 countries.

Russ Glennon is a Senior Lecturer in management and leadership at Nottingham Business School, Nottingham Trent University, UK. He is a council member of the British Academy of Management and chair of the Public Management & Governance special interest group. Prior to joining academia, he was a senior manager in local government.

Kirsten Greenhalgh is Associate Professor of Accounting and Chair of the School Teaching and Learning Committee at Nottingham University Business School, UK, and is also a member of the University's Quality

Standards Committee. Her professional background is in management accounting. She is a member of the Chartered Institute for Management Accountants and sits on their Adjudications Working Party. She held posts in the NHS and Local Government prior to joining academia.

LIST OF FIGURES

LIST OF TABLES

List of Tables

CHAPTER 1

But What Is Accountability?

Russ Glennon, Laurence Ferry,
Peter Murphy and Kirsten Greenhalgh

Abstract The genesis of this book originally derives from a report for the National Audit Office. This examined the government's ability to demonstrate the quality of service delivery in locally delivered public services in England, a responsibility, previously overseen by the former Audit Commission, between the 2010 and 2015 general elections. The Audit Commission formally closed on 31st March 2015 and part of its role transferred to the NAO. The report to the NAO provided a 'state of play' evaluation for the four areas of Local Government, Health and Social Care, the Police, and Fire and Rescue Services. It identified, adapted, and tested some of the dominant concepts of financial, service, and organisational accountability that had been applied and used in the contemporary UK context.

Keywords Accountability · Literature review · Conceptualisation

INTRODUCTION

The delivery of public services affects everyone on a daily basis, from quotidian services such as roads and refuse collections to those that we reach out to in our most vulnerable times, such as the police or ambulance services. Public service delivery is a fact of life.

We fund public services in a variety of ways, yet many of these ways are indirect—that is, not directly related to the 'consumption' of these

© The Author(s) 2019
P. Murphy et al., *Public Service Accountability*,
https://doi.org/10.1007/978-3-319-93384-9_1

1

services. Services differ but are largely funded via taxes collected locally and nationally. Some services, such as local government, have a direct democratic interface; for others, the lack of this feature is sometimes considered as a problem, often referred to as a 'democratic deficit'.

Sometimes, the public sector is referred to as if it were a single, homogenous block, often when compared with the private sector. Yet, it could be argued that more divergence exists within the public sector than between public and private. It could equally be argued that some processes and characteristics differ little: what makes effective leadership, management, and how to evaluate performance or financial expenditure may all have a high degree of similarity between organisations, services, or sectors.

However, we argue that the public sector is distinctive in the way that services are conceived, managed, and assessed. Too often the private sector operating model is taken as an ideal. This is the ethos behind New Public Management (Dunleavy and Hood 1994; Hood 1991, 1995): that the imposition of modern (competitive) business practices is the (best) way to encourage improvement in public service delivery.

We would argue that this is overly simplistic and reductive, particularly, when considering how public services are held to account. For example, if you are unhappy with the service, price, or quality provided in your preferred supermarket, there are several others that would be happy to accept your custom. You may not even have to travel far to find an alternative. Indeed, you do not have to limit yourself to one supermarket—you can do your shopping in as many as you choose, either in physical shops or online. If something isn't right, a complaint will usually secure you a replacement, refund, or in some cases, compensation for the inconvenience or disruption. Accountability, in these circumstances, is often interpreted as satisfaction on a transactional basis. The consumer may often take for granted the existence of regulations that ensure a safe service or product and may also rely on other consumers to aggregate their choices in such a way that the company delivers what is wanted, at a price that is acceptable, and to the desired level of innovation or design.

It can be argued that the private sector has introduced or facilitated many innovations that have improved public service delivery, from online reporting to performance management practices. And yet, the vast majority of public services are not like supermarket shopping or a restaurant meal. Simplistic accountability mechanisms that treat private and public sectors as being the same do both a disservice. The two sectors are perhaps 'alike in all unimportant respects' (Allison 1986).

At the same time, a body of the literature around what is termed 'co-production' or 'co-creation of value' (Radnor et al. 2014; Alford 2016; Lusch and Vargo 2006; Osborne et al. 2013) has begun to articulate the distinctiveness of a services-based approach, as opposed to product-based logics. This 'service-dominant logic' approach highlights the preponderance of the literature and perspectives rooted in the private sector; approaches that are too often uncritically presented as being significant for public services. This simplistic view also leans too heavily on a dyadic conception of services and products occurring at what Normann calls 'the moment of truth' (Normann 2000): that is, individual service interactions are what is important in delivering accountability, and the aggregation of those is sufficient to show that the organisation is working well. We will not revisit this argument here but rather suggest that this is one key part of developing a sense of how well public services are performing and will need to perform in the future. We will argue that purely backward-looking forms of reviewing service performance or failure are insufficient for public services (Haveri 2006). Accountability must also look forwards to create the environment for successful delivery, as well as review past performance.

The growing interest in co-production has helped to highlight some of the differences between co-producing an individual relationship with a service, and the impact on co-production (i.e. co-design, co-innovation) at a systemic level.

The same issue attaches to accountability. Service system accountability is deployed through regulatory mechanisms, which, since the global economic downturn of 2008 onwards, have been significantly dismantled in English public services in favour of pushing accountability down to citizens (Eckersley et al. 2014; Ferry et al. 2015; Ahrens and Ferry 2015; Ferry and Murphy 2015, 2018), perhaps reflecting Foucault's 'descending individualism' (Foucault 1991). We can see this in such mechanisms as the NHS's 'Friends and Family test', which asks people who have received medical treatment whether they would recommend the particular hospital department to people they know.

Thus, the dismantling or deregulation of service accountability has occurred alongside significant, but uneven, cuts in public expenditure (Ferry and Eckersley 2011, 2012, 2015b; Ferry and Murphy 2015, 2018). A cynic might suggest that the two are not hand-in-hand by coincidence, but nonetheless, public services are required to demonstrate that they are delivering services that are efficient, economic, and effective—the generally accepted definition of 'value for money' (Hopwood 1984).

How, might we ask, are bodies to do this in a deregulated, and challenging financial environment? How can we balance the individual/systemic approach, and the creation of the conditions for accountability? It is these questions that this book seeks to address through the development of a distinctive sense of *public service accountability*.

BACKGROUND

The genesis of parts of this book originally derives from a study and report for the National Audit Office (NAO) (Ferry and Murphy 2015). This examined the government's ability to demonstrate the financial sustainability and quality of service delivery in locally delivered public services previously overseen by the former Audit Commission (closed in 2015). The research explored the level of public assurance and the risks to services achieving value for money in 2010 and again in 2015. It looked at four types of public service organisations: local government, fire and rescue, the police, and health and social care. Hood's (2010) model of examining accountability and transparency, illustrating the relationship as one of 'Siamese twins', 'matching parts', or an 'awkward couple', was used as the primary frame to understand and evaluate the situation, building on a theoretical study of local government (Ferry et al. 2015).

The findings revealed that three of the four main public service organisations were actually *less* able to understand and demonstrate public assurance and value for money in 2015 when compared to their ability to do so in 2010. The extent of deterioration came as a surprise and the work provided an evidence base upon which to build for the NAO, academic audiences, and to a number of key stakeholders to whom subsequent presentations of the results were made, including the Local Government Association (LGA), the Centre for Public Scrutiny (CfPS), and the Chartered Institute of Public Finance and Accountancy (CIPFA).

The four organisations examined displayed, as we might expect, a range of responses and reactions to the strategic and operational challenges facing them. This complexity helped inform the perspective outlined in this book. Hood's (2010) framework was helpful in arriving at an understanding of the state of public service accountability, as well as serving to highlight additional questions worthy of further investigation. Rather than establish a normative process for defining accountability, however, this book seeks to develop an understanding of how accountability is being practised, and extract from that some thoughts and ideas for policy and practice.

STRUCTURE OF THE BOOK

The book is divided into three main parts. The first section encompasses this chapter and Chapter 2. The definition and theoretical explorations of accountability in academic literature are in this chapter. The development of an evaluative model is outlined in Chapter 2. In these two chapters, we lay out the foundations of accountability and discuss some of the numerous concepts that are intertwined with accountability, such as transparency, scrutiny, and public assurance.

The second section includes the four main empirical chapters. These explore each of the four public sector institutions (local government, fire and rescue, police, and health and social care) and examine their individual practices and features. In each of these four chapters, we reflect on the evaluative model and how the reality of accountability practices has developed in each area.

The third and final section brings together our conclusions across the four empirical chapters and raises some ideas for future research and implications for practice.

KEY CONCEPTS IN PUBLIC SERVICE ACCOUNTABILITY

Historically, accountability has been viewed as an obligation to provide an account to someone with a legitimate interest—a system of counting possessions and classifying this information. Its historical origins were formalised through the practice of bookkeeping and the discipline of accounting (Bovens et al. 2014a). However, the word has developed a wider political and cultural significance beyond those financial beginnings (Dubnick 2014) and can rightly be considered a cultural phenomenon.

As others have argued (e.g. Bovens et al. 2014b; Dubnick 2014; Hood 2002, 2006, 2007; Mulgan 2000; Sinclair 1995), accountability is polysemic—a 'chameleon' concept. It appears easily understood by the public, politicians, and academics alike, yet when financial and/or service failure occurs, and we start looking for people to hold to account, this shared understanding tends to come apart fairly easily. Few would argue for less accountability for public services, yet when we articulate accountability as, for example, a series of externally imposed rules, i.e. regulation, then this 'motherhood and apple pie' concept becomes less appealing to some at least. Accountability, it seems, is fine when it happens to other people, although everyone accepts that it is necessary. Bovens et al. (2014b) helpfully suggest we should consider accountability as *virtue* and accountability as *mechanism*; this is mirrored by Dubnick and Frederickson (2011) who provide a typology of accountability that embraces *instrumental* and *intrinsic* modes. These conceptual differences may help explain some of the difficulty in agreeing on the *what* and *how* of accountability, as well as the *why*.

There is, however, general agreement that public service accountability should be distinctive because *public* services are services funded by public money, delivered to and for the public. Thus, it seems, higher standards are often expected. We do not argue against this here. There has been sufficient study of the distinctiveness of the motivations of public servants (Perry and Wise 1990; Moynihan and Pandey 2007) and of the public (as opposed to private) value that the sector can and should deliver (Moore 1995; Williams and Shearer 2011) to accept that public services are different. Yet, this complexity is not always reflected in the literature and practices around accountability.

This problem emerges partly from differing theoretical positions on public services, and from adopting a bounded rationality with regard to definitions of what accountability is and what it means in practice. For example, democratic accountability is often held up as the 'gold standard' of accountability (Behn 2001; Radin 2006).

Clearly, the loss of an electoral mandate for service reform and change is a significant marker of public dissatisfaction with what has been achieved (or not), yet as a mechanism for controlling service delivery, council elections every three years, or general elections every five, are clearly inadequate on their own. And what happens in services where there is effectively little or no local democratic accountability, such as the NHS? Whilst, the current trend appears to be towards increasing local democratic accountability through, for example, the proposal to merge the governance of police and fire and rescue services under directly elected commissioners, or the changes to school governor roles and responsibilities, this dimension alone cannot be sufficient to explain or encapsulate public service accountability.

Thus, accountability requires a more subtle and granular understanding to establish the foundations on which further analysis can be undertaken. For many, this begins with principal/agent theory.

Lindberg provides a useful summary of the key aspects of accountability from the principal/agent theory perspective (Braun and Guston 2003; Gailmard 2014), where he describes the intellectual construction of accountability as requiring:

- An agent or institution who is to give an account (A for agent);
- An area, responsibilities, or domain subject to accountability (D for domain);
- An agent or institution to whom A is to give account (P for principal);
- The right of P to require A to inform and explain/justify decisions with regard to D; and
- The right of P to sanction A if A fails to inform and/or explain/justify decisions with regard to D (Lindberg 2013).

This perspective represents a sanctions-based model, which focuses on punishment, enacted through principal/agent theory. Whilst, this is not the only model for understanding accountability, it is a common one, certainly within public services scholarship (Behn 2001; Bovens et al. 2014a).

As a model, however, it is not without challenges. We suggest that two of these challenges are significant and related: the 'multiple principals, multiple goals' problem and the 'dyadic relationship' problem.

Private sector organisations with shareholders are accountable to those shareholders via organisational management. It can be argued that this superordinate responsibility to shareholders overrides or guides the others; this is the utilitarian argument. Indeed, this is Friedman's (1970) original concern. The management of the organisation should attempt to create and run a sustainable business in order to generate profit and thus ensure continued employment for staff; to reference *Star Trek*'s Mr. Spock, the needs of the many outweigh the needs of the few. Of course, this oversimplifies the relationship, but doing so also reduces it to its essential element. Whilst other stakeholders exist in the value chain, these are all subordinated to the primary characteristic—generating a profit-making, value-generating business for the owners of the equity in that business.

When we consider public services, the relationship is more complex. First, there are multiple principals in the accountability landscape, sometimes operating in clusters (Talbot 2008). Naturally, multiple principals also generate multiple goals and multiple accountabilities (Koppell 2005; Schillemans and Bovens 2011). Ostensibly, all public services are accountable to the political leadership at either a local or national level, depending on the service itself, as well as to the 'people', or *demos*. But these two are substantively different and require different forms of accountability mechanisms; beyond this, the politicians are in theory accountable to the people, but primarily via the ballot box, which even the most ardent supporters of democratic accountability would recognise is a rather blunt and costly instrument (Warren 2014).

This triadic accountability landscape (national political leadership, local political leadership, and the local population) is itself a simplification, and there are various challenges. Statutory public services fulfil a range of roles, from the direct provision of consumable, free-choice services such as leisure provision, universal services and public goods provision (e.g. roads), to targeted services, mandatory taxation collection, regulation and public protection, some of which ultimately result in denying people their liberty to protect themselves and others. The principals for such a broad remit must by definition be numerous and complex. Beyond this, public services are legally bound to serve anyone and everyone—be they residents, citizens, businesses, or visitors. This generates the potential for goal conflict (Wilson 2000).

Public service responsibilities are set out in numerous acts of parliament and statutory guidance. Some specific roles are prescribed in terms of what they must do, and what sort of person is allowed to do these roles, such as, say, a hospital 'Caldicott guardian' (patient confidentiality), 'safeguarding lead' (protection for children or vulnerable adults), or 'section 151 officer' (local government finance role). The statutory nature of some services also specifies the type, nature, and level of service in some regards. One example is the *Public Libraries and Museums Act* (1964), which specifies that '[i]t shall be the duty of every library authority to provide a comprehensive and efficient library service for all persons desiring to make use thereof'. Clearly, 'comprehensive' and 'efficient' require defining, but the act provides a benchmark against which performance may be understood. Thus, the challenge of multiple principals and multiple objectives introduces the need for complex accountabilities that are contingent on the key actors within the relevant domain, as well as the exogenous restrictions and requirements.

The second challenge we raise is that of the limitations of dyadic relationships. Within the field of management, it is well recognised that stakeholders are relatively easy to identify but that their relative salience is more difficult to establish (Mitchell et al. 1997). If we are to understand accountability as being contingent, this means moving beyond seeing accountability as the accumulation of individual, dyadic interactions and towards a systemic interpretation of accountability (and related governance) processes (Ferry and Ahrens 2017).

We suggest that accountability, therefore, needs to be understood in terms of three key characteristics:

- Accountabilities are multiple and contingent
- Accountability is forward-looking (prospective) as well as backward-looking (retrospective)
- Accountability must embrace both financial and service/performance accountability

We shall move on to consider the wider implications of accountability, before establishing the evaluative model in Chapter 2, where we also return to these three fundamental characteristics.

Romzek (2000) advances a model of accountability with four subtypes. These are: hierarchical, legal, political, and professional. Romzek argues that the four types coexist, and multiple presentations of differing accountability types can come into conflict. One weakness of Romzek's model is that it overlooks accountability to the public as a distinct grouping—this is surprising, given that her focus is on public service reform. She conflates 'the general public' into a wider group of stakeholders within political accountability—which is, as we said earlier, a rather blunt instrument. We suggest that services to the public represent the *sine qua non* of public management: i.e. without a public to serve, there would be no need for public management.

Sinclair (1995), writing from an Australian perspective, identifies five 'forms of accountability' in her research based upon chief executives of Australian public sector organisations. Sinclair's types include: political, managerial, public, professional, and personal.

Here legal accountability is replaced by personal—a sense of holding oneself to account against a moral or ethical code—what she refers to as 'personal conscience'. In UK, we could suggest the 'Nolan Principles' (Committee on Standards in Public Life 1995) as a framework for accountability that crosses the personal and professional divides. Although Sinclair suggests that accountability appears to defy definition and becomes fuzzier the more one attempts to do so, there are compelling reasons for scholars attempting to provide a typology of accountability, and both Romzek's and Sinclair's models contribute to this dialogue.

The original NAO report (Ferry and Murphy 2015), from which portions of this book emerged, examined ten-related concepts in terms of their application to the overarching process of accountability. These are listed below in bold, grouped into four headings.

- Accountability and transparency arrangements
- Data, information, and intelligence and interrogation and interpretation of information
- Governance, leadership and strategic alignment/co-delivery
- Public reporting, internal and external scrutiny and intervention regimes in the event of significant underperformance

In addition, potential value for money risks were identified for each public service institution. From this, key themes were derived and through comparative analysis commonalities and differences were highlighted.

In Table 1.1 we develop and summarise some of the key concepts and expand the conceptual framework to include a sense of related ideas. We also provide the description of our use of these concepts or ideas in this book.

We offer this not as an exhaustive list of concepts, but rather a summary of some of the concepts that become nested or entangled within accountability, which we propose here as the overarching concept through which the other concepts can be aligned.

Public Service Accountability as an Overarching Concept

As numerous academics have suggested, accountability is simultaneously simple to understand and complex to explain. For UK public services during the last 30 or so years, accountability was located in a financial paradigm, developed through financial accounting and into financial and

Table 1.1 Conceptual framework of accountability and related ideas

Developed concept	Selected academic support	Description
Accountability	Behn (2001), Romzek (2000), Sinclair (1995), Mulgan (2000), Lindberg (2013), Bovens et al. (2014a), Hood (2010), Eckersley et al. (2014), Ahrens and Ferry (2015), Ferry et al. (2015), Ferry and Eckersley (2015b)	The processes of holding to account—we argue for the use of accountability as an overarching concept
Accounting	Gray and Jenkins (1993), Jones and Pendlebury (2000), Broadbent and Guthrie (2008), Steccolini et al. (2017), Ferry et al. (2017, 2018), Ferry and Eckersley (2012, 2015b), Eckersley and Ferry (2011), Ahrens et al. (2018), Ahrens and Ferry (2015)	Financial management through reporting of expenditure against planned budgets—the basis on which much *accountability as mechanism* operates
Transparency	Birkinshaw (2006), Hood (2007, 2010), Ferry et al. (2015), Hood and Heald (2006), Ferry and Eckersley (2015a)	Openness and public sharing of information, often financial data. Viewed often as a *virtue*, but not always an effective *mechanism*
Systemic governance, leadership	Rhodes (1997), Stoker (1999), Osborne (2006), Radnor et al. (2016), Bao et al. (2012), Van Wart (2011), Allison (1986), Ferry and Ahrens (2017)	Developing systems of leadership of public services that enable accountability
Scrutiny/overview	Leach (2010), Wilson and Game (2011), Leach and Copus (2004), Kelly (2003), Murphy and Jones (2016)	Political processes whereby nonexecutive politicians examine and challenge the decisions of the executive decision-making bodies
Performance management, information management	Osborne et al. (1995), Bourne et al. (2000), Heinrich (2002), Broadbent and Laughlin (2009), Micheli and Mari (2014), Arnaboldi et al. (2015), Moynihan (2008), Martin et al. (2013), Ferry et al. (2018), Ahrens et al. (2018), Radin (2006)	Reporting of achievement against set goals and objectives, most commonly through numerical performance data

(continued)

Table 1.1   (continued)

Developed concept	Selected academic support	Description
Quality systems	Furterer and Elshennawy (2005), Pollitt (1990), Boyne et al. (2002), Burgess and Radnor (2013)	Established systems of assuring the quality of service planning and delivery, often via private sector inspired tools and techniques
Public assurance	Ferry and Murphy (2018), Gendron et al. (2001), Funnell and Wade (2012), Funnell (2011), Power (1994, 1997)	Explicit systems and processes to provide assurance that public funds are being appropriately spent
Co-production/co-creation of value, co-delivery	Osborne and Strokosch (2013), Radnor et al. (2014), Osborne et al. (2016)	Structured approaches to engaging service users in the design, delivery, innovation, and review of services
Probity, ethics	Greasley (2007), Maesschalck (2004), Committee on Standards in Public Life (1995), Sandford (2016)	Personal standards and behaviours
Regulation	Martin (2011), May (2007)	Externally imposed standards and requirements established in law or policy

subsequently performance audits and assessments (Ferry et al. 2017). This formalisation and development of regulatory mechanisms for capturing the performance or delivery of public services formed a key part of New Labour's *modernisation programme for local government* (Glennon et al. 2018). This developed into what Power (1994) originally referred to as an audit 'explosion', and subsequently termed 'rituals of verification' (Power 1997). Regulation of performance and audit was championed as a tool for strengthening accountability (Campbell-Smith 2008; Audit Commission and I&DeA 2002), although some critics of the regimes point to their negative impacts (Martin et al. 2010, 2013), including the cost of gathering the information as well as whether the schemes themselves represented value for money (Mayston 1993).

From the 1980s onwards, changes to the way in which public services were delivered, such as the increasing use of commissioning and contracting out, also led some scholars to classify the UK's public sector as a 'hollowed out' state (Rhodes 1997; Skelcher 2000). In a hollowed out public sector, the strictly hierarchical relationship between government and public service providers is increasingly replaced by more complex commercial, collaborative, and contractual relationships (Eckersley et al. 2014). This challenges the legitimacy of government and problematises the relationship between public employees and politicians or citizens (Skelcher 2000). It also necessitates a view of accountability that moves beyond the dyadic relationships of electorate/politician and the traditional public administration concern of the politics/administration dichotomy (Svara 2008).

Modern public services operate in a plural and pluralist context (Osborne 2010), where the policy and delivery domains have been 'unpacked' to allow (or enforce) access by multiple actors. Accountability itself as a concept is now central to the notion of democratic governance (Mulgan 2000); and accountability practices must reflect those changes. This would seem unambiguously positive: more people involved in the designing, governing, and delivery of public services should enhance the quality of all of those processes. This is captured by the emphasis on communities and community governance from New Labour (Stoker 2003; Skelcher 2004) and led to calls for the recognition of a New Public Governance (NPG) approach (Osborne 2006, 2010). Such an approach is evident in a range of mechanisms intended to empower users of public services and encourage bottom-up or *'downward'* accountability mechanisms (Denhardt and Aristigueta 2011; Denhardt and Denhardt 2015) which were visible in UK national policy under the New Labour governments (DCLG 2008). Thus, systemic accountability was deployed through regulatory mechanisms. These have since been largely dismantled in English public services (although not in Scotland), in favour of pushing accountability down to citizens via transparency initiatives such as 'armchair auditors' or performance measures such as the NHS 'Friends and Family Test'.

With continued reductions in public expenditure and increasing concerns around the financial sustainability of public services (NAO 2014, 2015a, b), the importance of accountability and transparency arrangements being 'fit for purpose' to provide public assurance and demonstrate value for money cannot be overestimated. Nowhere is this more so than in central and local government relations, where power and control are severely contested (Wildavsky 1964; Wilson and Game 2011).

We suggest that contemporary perceptions of the meanings associated with accountability have developed to include delivery *per*formance as well as financial *con*formance (Ferry and Eckersley 2015b).

Transparency in Public Services

In contrast to accountability, transparency champions openness as a means to prevent abuses of power, which has had a strong influence on democratic governance (Bovens et al. 2014a). Transparency refers to 'the conduct of business in a fashion that makes decisions, rules and other information visible from outside' (Hood 2010, p. 989). Despite a long history, it was not until the final decades of the twentieth century that the concept of transparency played a central role in the governance of both public and private organisations (Hood 2006). Mainstream political discourse characterises transparency as a normative good, and some scholars go so far as to even describe it as a human right (Birkinshaw 2006).

Hood (2010) focuses on answerability and thus contextualises accountability and transparency by referring to the multifaceted relationship between them as being like '*Siamese twins, matching parts and/or an awkward couple*'. '*Siamese twins*' suggests accountability and transparency are not wholly distinguishable. The tendency for both terms to be used interchangeably highlights this as a widely held interpretation. '*Matching parts*' suggests accountability and transparency are separable, but nevertheless complementary and both necessary for good governance, i.e. governments have to disclose some information to the public for democratic accountability. '*Awkward couple*' suggests accountability and transparency do not necessarily work together and there may be tension between them. This suggests increased transparency does not necessarily improve accountability or governance. For instance, the agent could publish volumes of poor-quality information the principal cannot easily access, interpret, or analyse.

Initially, i.e. after 2000, transparency was formalised in the UK public services through an opening up of archives, making minutes publicly available, and unlocking meetings for public attendance. This was to make information, data, and discussion more open and visible as part of transparency processes that support accountability. In recent decades, the prominence of transparency in the UK and elsewhere has increased through the development of technology, the Freedom of Information

Act (2000), Transparency International and other initiatives, and especially following the opportunities to share data and meetings online through the internet. The increase in data availability has been championed as a cost-effective means to afford a measure of accountability (DCLG 2011). However, it was also proposed as a response to the abolition of the Audit Commission (announced in early 2010, but not implemented until 2015) when so-called 'armchair auditors' would fill the gap left by the loss of the professional inspectorate. We discuss this further in Chapter 3.

One criticism of this form of financial transparency, and often of transparency policies in general, is that they do little other than generate huge amounts of data without facilitating meaningful analysis or interpretation. In the USA, citizens have not become the armchair auditors envisaged through transparency initiatives; it appears citizens simply did not have the time, money, expertise, or inclination to do so (Etzioni 2014).

This raises the question as to whether transparency can replace accountability. In the UK, there have been similar criticisms of transparency as a substitute for accountability and questions, in particular, about whether it is a suitable replacement for aspects of formalised audit (Ferry et al. 2015; Ferry and Eckersley 2015b). Empirical research from Portugal has also highlighted a failure to produce proper tools to compare government transparency practices (da Cruz et al. 2016). Although there are other international examples from China and India that show transparency can reinforce or even replace *inadequate* accountability mechanisms (Ferry and Eckersley 2015a).

It appears that while transparency can improve accountability in certain contexts, it may not in others (Ferry et al. 2015; Ferry and Eckersley 2015a). Heald (2006) argue we should value transparency instrumentally rather than intrinsically (e.g. as per Dubnick and Frederickson 2011) as a building block for other public policy benefits such as accountability, that it may support or counter. Transparency may not improve accountability if this data is merely published in order to tick a box or pay lip service to openness, or if it cannot be digested by stakeholders. In some cases, it may even generate adverse effects. Retrospective transparency has been justified in situations where contemporary transparency would be likely to lead to unintended consequences, perverse outcomes or, in cases such as emergencies, where contemporary or real-time transparency is impractical.

Transparency is often viewed as a prerequisite of accountability, because it gives the 'principal' access to potentially valuable data relating to their 'agent' (Hood 2010) and dissuades the government from acting inefficiently or oppressively (Birkinshaw 2006), particularly in contexts where public auditing processes may be underdeveloped or ineffective. We argue that transparency is best 'nested' within accountability as an overarching concept.

This risks being simplistic, however, because genuine accountability is contingent on the type and accessibility of data that are published, and whether recipients are able to understand them, and can access channels for complaint and enforce penalties in the event of malpractice (Hood and Heald 2006; Etzioni 2014; Ferry et al. 2015). In other words, the quality and type of data that are made available, as well as the capacity of their audience to analyse and understand them, may determine whether the principal can use them effectively for accountability purposes (Heald 2012). This suggests that transparency does not always increase public accountability and the two concepts are certainly not synonymous.

Whilst both transparency and accountability are seen as potential virtues that public services should champion and demonstrate, we have also acknowledged the importance of effective accountability mechanisms in ensuring that public services deliver what is needed and planned, and are able to demonstrate this (Bovens et al. 2014b). Simply professing the importance of accountability is insufficient—public services need to embrace creating the right conditions for accountability, and to understand the multiple, contingent nature of accountability mechanisms. It is these set of conditions that we address in Chapter 2, where we advance an evaluative model that emerged inductively from examining the practices of the four public services that form the subjects of chapters that follow.

Conclusion

This chapter has taken a reflective view on the definitions of accountability and related terms. It has shown that accountability has a broad conceptual footprint—it draws on a range of ideas and concepts, with much overlap between some of these. Accountability, we suggest, is best conceptualised as an overarching term under which the other concepts can be nested. We also suggest that governance, scrutiny, and culture are important features of the accountability paradigm, but that these should more properly be considered as contexts within which accountability operates, and thus will not be subject to detailed consideration here; we will leave that for a future work.

The focus, we wish to propose here is thus one of a *public service accountability* that is takes forward a more holistic conception of accountability, but that balances that with a structure than enables public organisations to reflect upon and develop accountability mechanisms, as well as reinforcing the underlying nature of accountability as a virtue. We therefore suggest that accountability can best be understood as having three key characteristics:

- Accountabilities are multiple and contingent
- Accountability is forward-looking (prospective) as well as backward-looking (retrospective)
- Accountability must embrace both financial and service/performance accountability.

In describing accountability as multiple and contingent here, we mean that accountability operates at both an individual and a systemic level and that must be a fundamental part of understanding the reality of accountability as practised by public service institutions, if we are to move beyond the limitations of principal/agent thinking. In order to advance this point, we now move on to develop an evaluative model to support this in Chapter 2.

REFERENCES

Ahrens, T., & Ferry, L. (2015). Newcastle City Council and the Grassroots: Accountability and Budgeting Under Austerity. *Accounting, Auditing & Accountability Journal, 28*(6), 909–933.

Ahrens, T., & Ferry, L. (2018). Institutional Entrepreneurship, Practice Memory, and Cultural Memory: Choice and Creativity in the Pursuit of Endogenous Change of Local Authority Budgeting. *Management Accounting Research, 38*, 12–21. https://doi.org/10.1016/j.mar.2016.11.001.

Ahrens, T., Ferry, L., & Khalifa, R. (2018). The Hybridising of Financial and Service Expertise in English Local Authority Budget Control: A Practice Perspective. *Qualitative Research in Accounting and Management* (Forthcoming).

Alford, J. (2016). Co-production, Interdependence and Publicness: Extending Public Service-Dominant Logic. *Public Management Review, 18*(5), 673–691.

Allison, G. T. (1986). Public and Private Administrative Leadership: Are They Fundamentally Alike in All Unimportant Respects. In *Leadership and Organizational Culture: New Perspectives on Administrative Theory and Practice* (pp. 214–222). Champaign: University of Illinois Press.

Arnaboldi, M., Lapsley, I., & Steccolini, I. (2015). Performance Management in the Public Sector: The Ultimate Challenge. *Financial Accountability & Management, 31,* 1–22.

Audit Commission, I&DeA. (2002). *Acting on Facts: Using Performance Measurement to Improve Local Authority Services.* London: Audit Commission.

Bao, G., Wang, X., Larsen, G. L., & Morgan, D. F. (2012). Beyond New Public Governance: A Value-Based GlobalFramework for Performance Management, Governance, and Leadership. *Administration & Society, 45,* 443–467.

Behn, R. D. (2001). *Rethinking Democratic Accountability.* Washington, DC: Brookings Institution Press.

Birkinshaw, P. (2006). Transparency as a Human Right. In *Proceedings-British Academy* (Vol. 135, pp. 47–58). Oxford: Oxford University Press.

Bourne, M., Mills, J., Wilcox, M., Neely, A., & Platts, K. (2000). Designing, Implementing and Updating Performance Measurement Systems. *International Journal of Operations & Production Management, 20,* 754–771.

Bovens, M., Goodin, R. E., & Schillemans, T. (2014a). *The Oxford Handbook of Public Accountability.* Oxford: Oxford University Press.

Bovens, M., Schillemans, T., & Goodin, R. E. (2014b). Public Accountability. In M. Bovens, R. E. Goodin, & T. Schillemans (Eds.), *The Oxford Handbook of Public Accountability* (pp. 1–22). Oxford: Oxford University Press.

Boyne, G. A., Gould-Williams, J. S., Law, J., & Walker, R. M. (2002). Best Value-Total Quality Management for Local Government? *Public Money and Management, 22,* 9–16.

Braun, D., & Guston, D. H. (2003). Principal-Agent Theory and Research Policy: An Introduction. *Science and Public Policy, 30*(5), 302–308. https://doi.org/10.3152/147154303781780290.

Broadbent, J., & Guthrie, J. (2008). Public Sector to Public Services: 20 Years of "Contextual" Accounting Research.*Accounting, Auditing & Accountability Journal, 21,* 129–169.

Broadbent, J., & Laughlin, R. (2009). Performance Management Systems: A Conceptual Model. *Management Accounting Research, 20,* 283–298.

Burgess, N., & Radnor, Z. (2013). Evaluating Lean in Healthcare. *International Journal of Health Care Quality Assurance, 26,* 220–235.

Campbell-Smith, D. (2008). *Follow the Money: A History of the Audit Commission.* London, UK: Penguin.

Committee on Standards in Public Life. (1995). *Standards in Public Life: First Report of the Committee on Standards in Public Life.* London.

da Cruz, N. F., Tavares, A. F., Marques, R. C., Jorge, S., & de Sousa, L. (2016). Measuring Local Government Transparency. *Public Management Review, 18*(6), 866–893.

DCLG. (2008). *Communities in Control: Real People, Real Power*. London: TSO.

DCLG. (2011). *Armchair Auditors Are Here to Stay*. London: HMG.

Denhardt, K. G., & Aristigueta, M. P. (2011). Performance Management Systems: Providing Accountability and Challenging Collaboration. In W. van Dooren & S. van de Walle (Eds.), *Performance Information in the Public Sector: How It Is Used*. Basingstoke: Palgrave Macmillan.

Denhardt, J. V., & Denhardt, R. B. (2015). *The New Public Service: Serving, Not Steering* (4th ed.). Abingdon: Routledge.

Dubnick, M. J. (2014). Accountability as a Cultural Keyword. In M. Bovens, R. E. Goodin, & T. Schillemans (Eds.), *The Oxford Handbook of Public Accountability* (pp. 23–38). Oxford: Oxford University Press.

Dubnick, M. J., & Frederickson, H. G. (Eds.). (2011). *Accountable Governance: Problems and Promises*. Abingdon: Routledge.

Dunleavy, P., & Hood, C. (1994). From Old Public Administration to New Public Management. *Public Money and Management, 14*(3), 9–16.

Eckersley, P. M., & Ferry, L. (2011). Budgeting and Governing for Deficit Reduction in the UK Public Sector: Act One'The Comprehensive Spending Review'. *Journal of Finance and Management in Public Services, 14–23*.

Eckersley, P., Ferry, L., & Zakaria, Z. (2014). A 'Panoptical' or 'Synoptical' Approach to Monitoring Performance? Local Public Services in England and the Widening Accountability Gap. *Critical Perspectives on Accounting, 25*(6), 529–538.

Etzioni, A. (2014). The Limits of Transparency. *Public Administration Review, 74*(6), 687–688. https://doi.org/10.1111/puar.12276.

Ferry, L., & Ahrens, T. (2017). Using Management Control to Understand Public Sector Corporate Governance Changes: Localism, Public Interest, and Enabling Control in an English Local Authority. *Journal of Accounting & Organizational Change, 13*(4), 548–567.

Ferry, L., & Eckersley, P. M. (2011). Budgeting and Governing for Deficit Reduction in the UK Public Sector: Act One 'the Comprehensive Spending Review'. *Journal of Finance and Management in Public Services, 10*(1), 14–23.

Ferry, L., & Eckersley, P. (2012). Budgeting and Governing for Deficit Reduction in the UK Public Sector: Act 2 'the Annual Budget'. *Public Money Manage, 32*(2), 119–126.

Ferry, L., & Eckersley, P. (2015a). Accountability and Transparency: A Nuanced Response to Etzioni. *Public Administration Review, 75*(1), 11–12.

Ferry, L., & Eckersley, P. (2015b). Budgeting and Governing for Deficit Reduction in the UK Public Sector: Act Three 'Accountability and Audit Arrangements'. *Public Money Manage, 35*(3), 203–210.

Ferry, L., Ahrens, T., & Khalifa, R. (2018). Public Value, Institutional Logics and Practice Variation During Austerity Localism at Newcastle City Council. *Public Management Review* (Forthcoming).

Ferry, L., Coombs, H., & Eckersley, P. (2017). Budgetary Stewardship, Innovation and Working Culture: Identifying the Missing Ingredient in English and Welsh Local Authorities' Recipes for Austerity Management. *Financial Accountability & Management, 33*(2), 220–243.

Ferry, L., Eckersley, P., & Zakaria, Z. (2015). Accountability and Transparency in English Local Government: Moving from 'Matching Parts' to 'Awkward Couple'? *Financial Accountability & Management, 31*(3), 345–361.

Ferry, L., & Murphy, P. (2015). *Financial Sustainability, Accountability and Transparency Across Local Public Service Bodies in England Under Austerity* (Report to National Audit Office (NAO)). London: National Audit Office.

Ferry, L., & Murphy, P. (2017). What About Financial Sustainability of Local Government!—A Critical Review of Accountability, Transparency, and Public Assurance Arrangements in England During Austerity. *International Journal of Public Administration, 41*(8), 619–629.

Foucault, M. (1991). *The Foucault Reader*, Rabinow, P. (Ed.). London: Penguin Books Ltd.

Friedman, M. (1970). The Social Responsibility of Business Is to Increase Its Profits. *The New York Times Magazine*.

Funnell, W. (2011). Keeping Secrets? Or what Government Performance Auditors Might not Need to know. *Critical Perspectives on Accounting, 22*, 714–721.

Funnell, W., & Wade, M. (2012). Negotiating the Credibility of Performance Auditing. *Critical Perspectives on Accounting, 23*, 434–450.

Furterer, S., & Elshennawy, A. K. (2005). Implementation of TQM and Lean Six Sigma Tools in Local Government: A Framework and a Case Study. *Total Quality Management & Business Excellence, 16*, 1179–1191.

Gailmard, S. (2014). Accountability and Principal/Agent Theory. In M. Bovens, R. E. Goodin, & T. Schillemans (Eds.), *The Oxford Handbook of Public Accountability* (pp. 90–105). Oxford: Oxford University Press.

Gendron, Y., Cooper, D. J., & Townley, B. (2001). In the Name of Accountability-State Auditing, Independence and New Public Management. *Accounting, Auditing & Accountability Journal, 14*, 278–310.

Glennon, R., Hodgkinson, I. R., Knowles, J., Radnor, Z., & Bateman, N. (2018). The Aftermath of Modernisation: Examining the Impact of a Change Agenda on Local Government Employees in the UK. *Australian Journal of Public Administration* (Forthcoming).

Gray, A., & Jenkins, B. (1993). Codes of Accountability in the New Public Sector. *Accounting, Auditing &Accountability Journal, 6.*

Greasley, S. (2007). Maintaining Ethical Cultures: Self-Regulation in English Local Government. *Local Government Studies, 33,* 451–464.

Haveri, A. (2006). Complexity in Local Government Change. *Public Management Review, 8*(1), 31–46. https://doi.org/10.1080/14719030500518667.

Heald, D. A. (2006). Varieties of Transparency. In *Transparency: The Key to Better Governance? Proceedings of the British Academy* (Vol. 135). Oxford: Oxford University Press.

Heald, D. (2012). Why Is Transparency About Public Expenditure so Elusive? *International Review of Administrative Sciences, 78*(1), 30–49.

Heinrich, C. J. (2002). Outcomes–Based Performance Management in the Public Sector: Implications for Government Accountability and Effectiveness. *Public Administration Review, 62,* 712–725.

Hood, C. (1991). A Public Management for All Seasons. *Public Administration, 69*(1), 3–19. https://doi.org/10.1111/j.1467-9299.1991.tb00779.x.

Hood, C. (1995). The New Public Management in the 1980s—Variations on a Theme. *Accounting, Organizations and Society, 20*(2–3), 93–109. https://doi.org/10.1016/0361-3682(93)E0001-W.

Hood, C. (2002). Control, Bargains and Cheating: The Politics of Public-Service Reform. *Journal of Public Administration Research and Theory, 12*(3), 309–332.

Hood, C. (2006). Gaming in Targetworld: The Targets Approach to Managing British Public Services. *Public Administration Review, 66*(4), 515–521.

Hood, C. (2007). Public Service Management by Numbers: Why Does It Vary? Where Has It Come from? What Are the Gaps and the Puzzles? *Public Money and Management, 27*(2), 95–102.

Hood, C. (2010). Accountability and Transparency: Siamese Twins, Matching Parts, Awkward Couple? *West European Politics, 33*(5), 989–1009.

Hood, C., & Heald, D. (2006). *Transparency: The Key to Better Governance?* (Vol. 135). Oxford: Oxford University Press for The British Academy.

Hopwood, A. (1984). Accounting and the Pursuit of Efficiency. In A. Hopwood & C. Tomkins (Eds.), *Issues in Public Sector Accounting.* Oxford: Philip Allan.

Jones, R., & Pendlebury, M. (2000). *Public Sector Accounting.* Harlow: Pearson Education.

Kelly, J. (2003). The Audit Commission: Guiding, Steering and Regulating Local Government. *Public Administration, 81,* 459–476.

Koppell, J. G. (2005). Pathologies of Accountability: ICANN and the Challenge of "Multiple Accountabilities Disorder". *Public Administration Review, 65*(1), 94–108.

Leach, S. (2010). The Audit Commission's View of Politics: A Critical Evaluation of the CPA Process. *Local Government Studies, 36,* 445–461.

Leach, S., & Copus, C. (2004). Scrutiny and the Political Party Group in UK Local Government: New Models of Behaviour. *Public Administration, 82,* 331–354.

Lindberg, S. I. (2013). Mapping Accountability: Core Concept and Subtypes. *International Review of Administrative Sciences, 79*(2), 202–226.

Lusch, R. F., & Vargo, S. L. (2006). Service-Dominant Logic: Reactions, Reflections and Refinements. *Marketing Theory, 6*(3), 281–288. https://doi.org/10.1177/1470593106066781.

Maesschalck, J. (2004). The Impact of New Public Management Reforms on Public Servants' Ethics: Towards a Theory. *Public Administration, 82,* 465–489.

Martin, S. (2011). Regulation. In R. Ashworth, G. Boyne, & T. Entwistle (Eds.), *Public Service Improvement: Theories and Evidence.* Oxford: OUP.

Martin, S., Downe, J., Grace, C., & Nutley, S. (2010). Validity, Utilization and Evidence-Based Policy: The Development and Impact of Performance Improvement Regimes in Local Public Services. *Evaluation, 16*(1), 31–42.

Martin, S., Downe, J., Grace, C., & Nutley, S. (2013). New Development: All Change? Performance Assessment Regimes in UK Local Government. *Public Money Manage, 33*(4), 277–280. https://doi.org/10.1080/09540962.2013.799816.

May, P. J. (2007). Regulatory Regimes and Accountability. *Regulation & Governance, 1,* 8–26.

Mayston, D. (1993). Principals, Agents and the Economics of Accountability in the New Public Sector. *Accounting, Auditing & Accountability Journal, 6*(3).

Micheli, P., & Mari, L. (2014). The Theory and Practice of Performance Measurement. *Management Accounting Research, 25,* 147–156.

Mitchell, R. K., Agle, B. R., & Wood, D. J. (1997). Toward a Theory of Stakeholder Identification and Salience: Defining the Principle of Who and What Really Counts. *Academy of Management Review, 22*(4), 853–886.

Moore, M. H. (1995). *Creating Public Value: Strategic Management in Government.* Cambridge: Harvard University Press.

Moynihan, D. P. (2008). *The Dynamics of Performance Management: Constructing Information and Reform.* Washington, DC: Georgetown University Press.

Moynihan, D. P., & Pandey, S. K. (2007). The Role of Organizations in Fostering Public Service Motivation. *Public Administration Review, 67*(1), 40–53.

Mulgan, R. (2000). 'Accountability': An Ever-Expanding Concept? *Public Administration, 78*(3), 555–573.

Murphy, P., & Jones, M. (2016). Building the Next Model for Intervention and Turnaround in Poorly Performing Local Authorities in England. *Local Government Studies, 42*, 698–716.

NAO. (2014). *Financial Sustainability of Local Authorities.* London: National Audit Office.

NAO. (2015a). *Financial Sustainability of Police Forces in England and Wales.* London: National Audit Office.

NAO. (2015b). *Sustainability and Financial Performance of Acute Hospital Trusts.* London: National Audit Office.

Normann, R. (2000). *Service Management: Strategy and Leadership in Service Business* (3rd ed.). Chichester: Wiley.

Osborne, S. P. (2006). The New Public Governance? *Public Management Review, 8*(3), 377–387. https://doi.org/10.1080/14719030600853022.

Osborne, S. P. (Ed.). (2010). *The New Public Governance? Emerging Perspectives on the Theory and Practice of Public Governance.* Abingdon: Routledge.

Osborne, S. P., & Strokosch, K. (2013). It takes Two to Tango? Understanding the Co-production of Public Services by Integrating the Services Management and Public Administration Perspectives. *British Journal of Management, 24*, S31–S47.

Osborne, S. P., Radnor, Z., & Nasi, G. (2013). A New Theory for Public Service Management? Towards a (Public) Service-Dominant Approach. *American Review of Public Administration, 43*(2), 135–158.

Osborne, S. P., Radnor, Z., & Strokosch, K. (2016). Co-Production and the Co-Creation of Value in Public Services: A Suitable Case for Treatment? *Public Management Review, 18*, 639–653.

Osborne, S. P., Bovaird, T., Martin, S., Tricker, M., & Waterston, P. (1995). Performance Management and Accountability in Complex Public Programmes. *Financial Accountability & Management, 11*, 19–37.

Perry, J. L., & Wise, L. R. (1990). The Motivational Bases of Public Service. *Public Administration Review, 50*(3), 367. https://doi.org/10.2307/976618.

Pollitt, C. (1990). Doing Business in the Temple-Managers and Quality Assurance in the Public-Services. *Public Administration, 68*, 435–452.

Power, M. (1994). *The Audit Explosion* (Vol. 7). London: Demos.

Power, M. (1997). *The Audit Society: Rituals of Verification.* Oxford: Oxford University Press.

Radin, B. A. (2006). *Challenging the Performance Movement: Accountability, Complexity and Democratic Values.* Washington, DC: Georgetown University Press.

Radnor, Z., Osborne, S., & Glennon, R. (2016). Public Management Theory. In C. Ansell & J. Torfing (Eds.),*Handbook on Theories of Governance.* Cheltenham: Edward Elgar.

Radnor, Z., Osborne, S. P., Kinder, T., & Mutton, J. (2014). Operationalizing Co-production in Public Services Delivery: The Contribution of Service Blueprinting. *Public Management Review, 16*(3), 402–423.

Rhodes, R. A. W. (1997). *Understanding Governance: Policy Networks, Governance, Reflexivity and Accountability.* Buckingham: Open University Press.

Romzek, B. S. (2000). Dynamics of Public Sector Accountability in an Era of Reform. *International Review of Administrative Sciences, 66,* 21–44.

Sandford, M. (2016). *Local Government Standards in England* [Online]. London: House of Commons Library. [Accessed 05/01/2018].

Schillemans, T., & Bovens, M. (2011). The Challenge of Multiple Accountability. In M. J. Dubnick & H. G. Frederickson (Eds.), *Accountable Governance: Problems and Promises.* Abingdon: Routledge.

Sinclair, A. (1995). The Chameleon of Accountability: Forms and Discourses. *Accounting, Organizations and Society, 20*(2/3), 219–237.

Skelcher, C. (2000). Changing Images of the State: Overloaded, Hollowed-Out, Congested. *Public Policy and Administration, 15*(3), 3–19.

Skelcher, C. (2004). The New Governance of Communities. In G. Stoker & D. Wilson (Eds.), *British Local Government into the 21st Century* (pp. 25–43). Basingstoke: Palgrave Macmillan.

Steccolini, I., Jones, M., & Salterer, I. (Eds.). (2017). *Governmental Financial Resilience: International PerspectivesOn How Local Government Faces Austerity.* Bingley: Emerald.

Stoker, G. (Ed.). (1999). *The New Management of British Local Governance.* Basingstoke: Palgrave.

Stoker, G. (2003). *Transforming Local Governance: From Thatcherism to New Labour.* Basingstoke: Palgrave Macmillan.

Svara, J. H. (2008). Beyond Dichotomy: Dwight Waldo and the Intertwined Politics-Administration Relationship. *Public Administration Review, 68*(1), 46–52.

Talbot, C. (2008). Performance Regimes—The Institutional Context of Performance Policies. *International Journal of Public Administration, 31*(14), 1569–1591.

Van Wart, M. (2011). *Dynamics of Leadership in Public Services.* New York: ME Sharpe Inc.

Warren, M. E. (2014). Accountability and Democracy. In M. Bovens, R. E. Goodin, & T. Schillemans (Eds.), *The Oxford Handbook of Public Accountability* (pp. 39–54). Oxford: Oxford University Press.

Wildavsky, A. B. (1964). *Politics of the Budgetary Process.* Boston: Little Brown.

Williams, I., & Shearer, H. (2011). Appraising Public Value: Past, Present and Futures. *Public Administration, 89*(4), 1367–1384.

Wilson, D., & Game, C. (2011). *Local Government in the United Kingdom* (5th ed.). London: Palgrave Macmillan.

Wilson, J. Q. (2000). *Bureaucracy: What Government Agencies Do and Why They Do It*. New York: Basic Books.

CHAPTER 2

Our Evaluative Model

Russ Glennon, Laurence Ferry and Peter Murphy

Abstract In this chapter, we revisit the evaluative model used for the NAO report to try to develop and apply an enhanced evaluative model. In order to do this, we focus on four key questions: what governance mechanisms are in place; what must the system in England deliver; what external regulation and scrutiny currently contribute to the regime; and what are the funding arrangements and their consequences. The analysis also highlighted two sets of tensions: individual and systemic/collective approaches to accountability, and retrospective and prospective accountability. The new model seeks to synthesise these two dimensions and accepting the specific configuration of accountability is service and context specific, we suggest some principles or propositions for designing accountability into effective public service delivery.

Keywords Individual · Systemic · Prospective · Retrospective Accountability

As chapter 1 outlines, accountability is something of a 'motherhood and apple pie' concept: broadly understood by most, but very difficult to pin down to an exact definition. Accountability is thus coded with different layers of meanings (polysemy) and values in differing contexts. Its polysemic, contingent nature thus provides a challenge for practitioners and scholars when attempting to both understand what accountability is and

© The Author(s) 2019   27
P. Murphy et al., *Public Service Accountability*,
https://doi.org/10.1007/978-3-319-93384-9_2

evaluate whether or how well it has occurred. Even beyond this barrier, what we might term 'mythical' (Gray and Jenkins 1995), 'symbolic', or 'ritualistic' codes of accountability can operate whereby the processes of accountability practices are enacted but there is little resulting change. We would argue that these additionally problematise the study and implementation of accountability. And neither should accountability be seen as a dichotomous variable. There are clear variations in effectiveness, depth, and sophistication within practices.

This chapter, therefore, seeks to develop a high-level evaluative model. Such a model cannot hope to be all-encompassing, but it can provide a pragmatic basis from which the remaining empirical chapters can be better understood and hopefully inform future practical developments in policy formulation, service delivery, and public assurance.

An earlier evaluative model that formed the basis of the assessment and reports to the National Audit Office (NAO) (Ferry and Murphy 2015) was based upon earlier academic literature (e.g., Ferry et al. 2015; Hood 2010) and non-academic (principally official and regulatory) literature. It identified, adapted, and tested some of the dominant concepts relating to financial, service, and organisational accountability that have been applied and used in the UK context.

The review initially identified nine relevant evaluative concepts, expanded to ten during the course of the research process. Some of these concepts clearly overlap with others and some are interdependent on each other. However, these ten concepts were used to evaluate the financial and performance regime in the four public service institutions—local government, police, fire, and health and social care—that appeared in subsequent presentations and reports to the key stakeholders, academic and non-academic interested parties, and the commissioners, the NAO. Those ten concepts were:

- Accountability
- Transparency
- Governance
- Leadership
- Strategic alignment/co-delivery/collaborative delivery
- Information/performance management
- Interrogation and interpretation tools available
- Public reporting
- Internal and external scrutiny
- Intervention regime (in the event of significant underperformance)

We highlighted these ten concepts in Chapter 1 and we will not go back over them here. Rather, the aim is to develop a better understanding of the ways in which evaluation can be seen from a systemic perspective. These ten concepts were helpful in reviewing those services at that time. However, since that work, we have reconceptualised accountability driven by the need to develop a new evaluative model. As we articulate later, this model is not a normative or prescriptive one, but rather one that emerges from the reality of accountability practices as observed through a range of empirical data gathering across a range of service areas.

As we outlined in Chapter 1, conceptual advances in thinking around the context of service delivery, including New Public Governance, Public Value, and public service dominant logics, have begun to shift our understanding of how accountability might operate in public service environments. They enable us to be clearer about some of the challenges inherent in *public service accountability.*

As Chapter 1 has demonstrated, accountability has a broad conceptual footprint, encompassing a plethora of terms and concepts. This perhaps leads to an excessive focus on whether or not accountability has been achieved within some of the academic and practitioner literature. Again, here, the distinction between accountability as *mechanism* and as *virtue* (Bovens et al. 2014) is helpful. Dubnick (2014) also considers accountability as a cultural keyword. Similarly, the inherent layers of meaning associated with accountability as a term facilitate differing ways in which those meanings can be interpreted; one person's accountability is another's excessive control. This, then, influences views as to whether accountability is achieved, delivered, or even performed. We also suggest here that governance, scrutiny, and perhaps culture are better understood as part of the context of how accountability operates, whereas transparency, for example, is a component of accountability mechanisms. Thus, we will not focus in this book on those aspects; there are plenty of excellent discussions of these aspects elsewhere.

In order to provide a route for understanding the reality of accountability practices, we have articulated three key elements in Chapter 1:

- Accountabilities are multiple and contingent (embracing individual and systemic forms)
- Accountability is forward-looking (prospective) as well as backward-looking (retrospective)
- Accountability must embrace both financial and service/performance accountability

The first two of these key points develop into two primary continua: individual versus systemic accountability, and prospective and retrospective accountability. We will now discuss both sets of elements and attempt to integrate these two continua to further develop the model.

Individual Versus Systemic Accountability

In 1994, the government set up the Committee on Standards in Public Life, led by Lord Nolan to act as an independent committee advising the government on ethical issues and standards. A year later, this committee published a set of seven principles for public life (Committee on Standards in Public Life 1995).

These seven 'Nolan principles' are primarily aimed at the ethical conduct of individuals in public life, i.e. members of parliament, civil or public servants, and so on. They remain a significant contribution to the debate around accountability, with this specifically being one of the seven standards (Table 2.1).

Table 2.1   The Nolan principles

Standard	Description
1. Selflessness	Holders of public office should act solely in terms of the public interest
2. Integrity	Holders of public office must avoid placing themselves under any obligation to people or organisations that might try inappropriately to influence them in their work. They should not act or take decisions in order to gain financial or other material benefits for themselves, their family, or their friends. They must declare and resolve any interests and relationships
3. Objectivity	Holders of public office must act and take decisions impartially, fairly and on merit, using the best evidence and without discrimination or bias
4. Accountability	Holders of public office are accountable to the public for their decisions and actions and must submit themselves to the scrutiny necessary to ensure this
5. Openness	Holders of public office should act and take decisions in an open and transparent manner. Information should not be withheld from the public unless there are clear and lawful reasons for so doing
6. Honesty	Holders of public office should be truthful
7. Leadership	Holders of public office should exhibit these principles in their own behaviour. They should actively promote and robustly support the principles and be willing to challenge poor behaviour wherever it occurs

Here we see one of the primary tensions in accountability: the difference between individual and systemic accountability. Traditional principal/agent theory rests heavily on individual accountability, driven by external forces, as shown in Chapter 1. This type of accountability also features in public conceptions of accountability, i.e. 'the court of public opinion' or a public/media desire to see 'heads roll' for public service failures.

Whilst individual accountability and the demands for punishments also exist in the private sector, the reliance on public funding and the higher standards of probity and individual ethical behaviour expected from the public sector do characterise it as having a distinctive nature (Warren 2014). This locates accountability within democracy and thus characterises accountability as a moral concept. Denhardt and Denhardt (2015, p. ix) argue that 'public servants do not deliver customer service, they deliver democracy' and this positioning of public service within moral and democratic values clearly forms part of the literature on public service motivation (Perry and Wise 1990; Moynihan and Pandey 2007) as well as public administration (Bovens et al. 2014 provide a useful summary of these positions). But public servants demonstrably *do* deliver services to customers, and when they do so they may increasingly be delivering on behalf of public institutions as outsourced staff. Individual and service interactions remain fundamental to the wider public (and media) perceptions of how and why services should be accountable.

As we know, service interactions are conducted in the context of institutional and systemic processes that the individual public service provider, be that a police officer, nurse, or housing manager, rarely has control over. At what service theory calls 'the moment of truth' (Normann 2000), these individuals are enacting policies and processes set across the organisation, inevitably with limited discretion. Legislation and established practices closely frame the delivery of public services: for example, the *Police and Criminal Evidence Act (1984)* for the police service, democratic schemes of delegation for local government, risk management and assessment practices for the fire and rescue service, and the Hippocratic oath for the NHS, to name but a few. Thus, if we are to fully embrace a model of accountability that is effective in critiquing public services, we need to understand accountability as being both individual and systemic in nature.

In addition, public services (and individuals within those services) are subject to scrutiny, overview, inspection, and direction

from external sources. From a classical Public Administration perspective (Svara 2008; Chandler 2000; Bovens et al. 2014), this often
returns to questions of responsiveness to the electorate. We contend
that political accountability—from local service institutions to (political) central government, from central government to the electorate,
and from local service institutions to the local electorate—is essential
for overall accountability at a higher level. This may perhaps operate in
a Foucauldian sense of self-disciplining (Foucault1991, 1977), i.e. the
knowledge that at some point decision-makers will be held accountable
at the ballot box for the impact of their decisions. We also contend,
however, that this is a necessary but insufficient component to facilitate
accountability, particularly at the operational level (Ahrens and Ferry
2015; Eckersley et al. 2014).

Whilst chapter 1 developed our key concepts, this chapter also builds
on our own retrospective critique of the earlier model. This has led to
lessons upon which we have reflected in the recommendations in our
final chapter.

In order to be able to develop and apply an improved evaluative
model, we must first understand the differing nature of the four local
public service types we discuss later in the book, i.e. local government,
health, police forces, and fire and rescue services. Each contains distinctive organisational components that mutually reinforce and influence the
nature of accountability mechanisms. From an organisational perspective,
then, the analytical model is built upon four key questions:

- What are the governance mechanisms in place to provide leadership
  management and crucially internal scrutiny and oversight?
- What level of local discretion exists in how the service is configured
  and delivered, and what are the things it must deliver?
- What external regulation or inspection is there—and does this contribute to public assurance, service improvement, and organisational
  development?
- What are the funding mechanisms, and what balance of central/
  local funding exists?

Firstly, we ask what the relevant governance mechanisms in place are.
Fundamentally, this question addresses the topic of who sets the direction for the service at the local level. Clearly, central government drives

the political agenda in the matter of longer-term delivery of outcomes, but what mechanisms exist that provide a level of internal scrutiny and oversight for local delivery against those overarching objectives?

Secondly, what flexibility is there in how services are configured, and priorities set? Each of the four main public service organisations discussed below has their own individual overriding objectives. Between 1998 and 2009 they were explicitly articulated and derived from successive sets of 'public service agreements' (PSAs) established by central government. Local government, for example, is responsible for improving the economic, social, and environmental well-being of the local area (DCLG 2011b; DTLR 2000). But what does this mean in reality? The needs, demands, and priorities of, say, Windsor and Maidenhead will be clearly different from those of Newcastle or Cornwall.

Whilst politicians may exhort approaches such as payment by results, and 'what matters is what works', financial auditing and accounting mechanisms very much reject a utilitarian approach that focuses on end results alone. Indeed, from an accounting perspective it often seems that money should be spent properly and wisely, but most definitely in that order. This could be argued to be a false dichotomy. When service failures occur, reasons for poor performance may be myriad and require a clear outlining of what level of performance was anticipated as being acceptable. Compliance with contracting rules and financial standing orders is much less open to interpretation and is ontologically much less complex, although recent experiences with high-profile outsourced services such as G4S, Carillion, and Capita may suggest that even these rules may not be applied effectively if political ambitions overrule contractual rigour.

The third component that we consider essential to understanding the accountability context is external audit, inspection, and regulation. The coalition government of 2010–2015 announced the abolition of the Audit Commission, the primary regulatory body for local government, in 2010 (although, it took until 2015 to finally close it) whilst regulators for health and social care and education have continued throughout that period, albeit with revised remits, scope, and objectives. Police and crime commissioners were introduced to establish a more political perspective on local policing and crime matters, though 'local' here means police force rather than local authority or political constituency level. Recent events and legislation (Home Office 2017) have seen moves to bring together the governance of police and fire and rescue services, often referred to as 'blue light integration', via the government's preferred model of police, fire, and crime commissioners. Fire and rescue services and police forces have reinstated and/or refreshed external inspection regimes, although at the time of writing the form of fire and rescue inspection is unclear and subject to consultation. We consider how closely regulated these locally delivered public services are.

Finally, the perennial notion of funding remains a pivotal concern for accountability. Stewardship of public finances is often seen as accepting responsibility for resources from a principal (Gray and Jenkins 1993; Stewart 2000).

In 1983, the accountability and stewardship of public money underwent fundamental change (Dewar and Funnell 2017). These changes established the Audit Commission, reframed the NAO, and placed the 3 E's of economy, efficiency, and effectiveness at the heart of the English assessment and audit regime, as well as devolving audit responsibilities to Scotland and Wales. This fundamentally influenced the nature and operation of audit and inspection up until 2015. From this period, the in-depth examination of effectiveness resolved previous tensions around the questioning of national or local policy. Accountability for delivering results and for using resources appropriately became inextricably linked and fundamental to our concept of public service accountability.

Table 2.2 summarises the position of the four local public service organisations we examine and outlines the major features of each against our four key questions.

We now move on to consider the second continuum that is essential to understanding public service accountability: retrospective and prospective accountability mechanisms.

RETROSPECTIVE AND PROSPECTIVE ACCOUNTABILITY MECHANISMS

As we have discussed, accountability works at both the individual and the systemic levels. There is also a relationship between these two levels—each does not stand alone, but neither does systemic accountability merely result from the aggregation of individual accountabilities. Here we address what Bovens et al. (2014) describe as 'accountability as mechanism'.

Table 2.2   Comparison of four local service institutions

Institution	Governance mechanisms	Level of local discretion	External regulation	Service funding mechanisms
Local government	Directly elected political control responsible for all services, resources, and priorities	Some external standards and statutory responsibilities, but significant freedom to design and deliver services (power of general competence) Highly localised	No organisational-level regulation. Some services regulated by individual government departments and agencies, e.g. Ofsted, CQC Lightly regulated	Funded through revenue support grant, local council tax, national non-domestic rates, and charges and fees for services Controlled and restricted by C Government
NHS (local trusts)	No direct political control, but strong central and organisational oversight, with independent trustee boards with user and staff representation at local level	National standards in key areas, as well as clinical standards. Strong direction from NHS centre, but freedom to innovate	External regulation and inspection from CQC, often focused on service failure Lightly regulated	NHS annual settlement via Department of Health, driven through commissioning between tiers (acute, CCG etc.)
Police	Directly elected PCCs responsible for strategic resource management and priorities	Strong external standards. Predominantly centrally controlled, but with scope for local prioritisation	Historically HMIC have been very close to the Home Office. The new HMICFRS inspectorate regime established 2012 is merely a continuation of existing arrangements for the police Closely regulated	Funded through central government grant and local precepting of council tax
Fire and Rescue Service	Still mainly FRA although in transition—no universal system of direct political control but current plans to integrate with PCCs	Strong external standards. Mainly centrally controlled, but with scope for local prioritisation	Previous inspectorate abolished. Developing new inspectorate regime (HMICFRS) A new regime and increasing degree of regulation likely	Funded through central government grant (as part of LG grant settlement) local precepting of council tax

Accountability structures operate both to establish the parameters of accountability, and to provide the means for demonstrating accountability. We have termed these two defining characteristics as 'prospective accountability' and 'retrospective accountability'. Clearly, there is, or should be, a relationship between these two.

This may be implicit in the principal/agent relationship, i.e. something is delegated to an agent to deliver. Yet this is simplistic, given that public services are complex, increasingly multi-agency entities. Even when these expectations are made explicit in legislation, their interpretation and operationalisation are problematic. The public to which services are delivered will differ from area to area, and within or across the same area. Local discretion and political priorities exists, at least in local government, police, and now fire and rescue services, through directly elected representatives. Whilst the NHS had not by 2015 been subjected to *local* politicisation in the same way, the provision of its services is subject to variation and variability in demand, and there have been accusations of 'weaponising' the NHS, i.e. using service failures as an instrument to generate political capital. And at the same time, each of the four service institutions has statutory activities, which are unlikely to vary from one year to another, and discretionary activities that may well differ.

An effective model of accountability, therefore, must rest upon appropriate mechanisms to specify the future level of service/outcomes expected. It must also provide assurance around the likely effectiveness of the service in delivering those outcomes, including appropriateness of expenditure, and provide effective governance to do so. It should also provide a framework through which performance and expenditure can be assessed. Established expectations thus clearly bound the discretion/control trade-off of accountability.

The corollary of this should then be a series of opportunities for the institution to analyse, evaluate, and understand their performance, as well as the opportunity to explore or expect corrective action to be taken. This might also include meeting targets, standards, or regulations with transparent reporting of performance, perhaps with an overall evaluative label, such as a 'star rating'. From the political perspective, this might also include checking compliance with political objectives, targets, or preferences, and the achievement of political aims that mirror some of the service aims.

Table 2.3 outlines some of the more common tools used for both prospective and retrospective accountability mechanisms.

Table 2.3 Prospective and retrospective accountability

Tools for creating accountability frameworks	*Tools for demonstrating accountability performance*
Plans, strategies, policies	Internal and external reporting of financial
Evidence base	and operational performance
Needs assessment	
'Contractual' forms such as local public service agreements	
External standards and benchmarks	Audit
Quality standards	Self-assessment
Contracts and contractual forms	Contract monitoring
National policy ambitions and goals	Intervention
Governance mechanisms	External rating, e.g. star ratings, league tables, etc.
Inspection (including peer review) for improvement	Inspection (including peer review) for compliance
Prospective	*Retrospective*

New institutions set up to implement these new arrangements included Foundation Trusts and a rebranded and refocussed regulatory body entitled 'NHS Improvement' in the NHS. Her Majesty's Inspectorate of Constabulary has been revitalised and police and crime commissioners introduced in criminal justice; free schools and a new school governor competency framework in education have been established, and a new national framework and standards body for fire and rescue. The biggest change, however, was the abolition of the Audit Commission. The commission had previously assessed and supported accountability and assurance in all locally delivered public services, including the four organisations discussed in the following chapters. The Audit Commission's supposed replacement, an army of so-called armchair auditors made up of members of the public (DCLG 2011a), has yet to emerge.

Having discussed individual and systemic levels of accountability, and retrospective and prospective mechanisms of accountability, we will consider how they interact in our evaluative model.

EVALUATIVE MODEL

Chapter 1 discussed the fundamental components and understanding of accountability in more general terms. However, accountability is highly polysemic and contextually contingent. If theoretical discussions of accountability are to provide better tools and techniques to improve public service accountability, then we need to move beyond theoretical concepts and develop an understanding of how accountability operates at the applied level within public services.

Earlier in this chapter, we established four key questions to enable a better understanding of the four local public service institutions: local government, police, fire and rescue, and health and social care.

This analysis has also charted two sets of tensions: individual and systemic/collective approaches to accountability, and retrospective and prospective mechanisms, and our model of evaluating accountability seek to synthesise these two dimensions. We have integrated these two continua into a model that establishes four primary modes of accountability practices, though we do not suggest that each category below is discrete and limiting. Organisations within the four local public service institutions are heterogeneous and may even demonstrate differences between individual business or service units. Our aim is to use this model to illustrate the sorts of choices made or imposed on services when it comes to accountability; to draw out themes, patterns, and contradictions in how the four different public service institutions may be treated by central government, and to arrive at conclusions as to how pragmatic improvements in accountability may be generated within and between the four public service institutions.

The model below will be used to draw out conclusions and observations in the next four chapters, and bring these together in the final chapter, where we consider what the design principles for effective accountability might look like.

Table 2.4 outlines the four modes of accountability practices within our evaluative model.

This model provides four modes of accountability practices. These are not meant to be mutually exclusive, but rather to express the primary focus and tools used to establish and demonstrate accountability within the local public service institutions. It then leads us to explore what balance of these four modes exists in each of the institutions.

Mode One: Service Management (Individual and Retrospective Focus)

In this mode of accountability, the primary concern is to examine service failures at the individual or micro-level in terms of customer service failure. Accountability here often tends towards granular or atomistic

Table 2.4 Four modes of accountability

		Nature of accountability mechanisms (Focus)	
		Retrospective	*Prospective*
Level of accountability (Locus)	*Systemic/collective*	*Mode two (institutional comparison)* League tables, inspection ratings Performance reporting Self-assessment Inspections	*Mode three (facilitating continuous improvement)* Governance changes Inspecting for improvement Plans and strategies Needs assessment Contracts
	Individual	*Mode one (service management)* Quality auditing Holding to account for individual service failures after they have occurred (complaints) Performance management More operational co-production approaches	*Mode four (service design)* Service design, co-design, co-production Quality standards and benchmarks Participatory budgeting and individual social care budgets

practices, often stimulated by the implementation of performance management, driven by target regimes. Such approaches may be open to 'gaming' (Bevan and Hood 2006; Radnor 2011), leading to delivery that meets the requirements of auditing or systems, but not necessarily the needs or expectations of service users. However, this mode provides a clear basis on which judgements are made that is auditable and understandable—targets are either achieved, or they are not.

Mode Two: Institutional Comparison (Systemic/Collective and Retrospective Focus)

This mode has been extensively used by the 1997–2010 New Labour administrations, as well as others, and still remains a key feature in public service management. In this mode, inspections and nationally generated league tables and suchlike are used to compare individual organisations against each other. Such efforts rely on the application of national standards, the outcomes of which are ranked and rated in a reductive process that simplifies the complexity of public service delivery to a single word (e.g. the use of terms such as *excellent* or *weak* for local government, or for health and social care, 'star ratings'). Given the relative difficulty with which individual users of services can switch provider, it is hard to place much credence in the relevance of these reductive labels for informing public service choice. Similarly, individual service failures are unlikely to stimulate a reduction in label category. However, it should be recognised that these labels have arguably been considered more worthwhile by the public in the case of schools and, to a lesser extent, hospitals. They are also accessible in terms of wider public understanding, even if the detail of what is implicit in a 'weak council' is opaque.

Mode Three: Facilitating Continuous Improvement (Systemic/ Collective and Prospective)

The continuous improvement mode addresses prospective or forward-looking capacity to deliver enhanced service levels. Operations in this mode include changes to governance structures and institutional capacity and the setting of long-term strategies and plans, as well as what we term 'inspection for improvement', as opposed to 'inspection for compliance', which forms part of mode two. Mode three may draw upon performance management techniques, but in ways that are distinct from mode two, where the dominance of targets over achievement (Hood 2006, 2007) and attempts to construct an artificially constructed line of strategic integration—the so-called golden thread (Micheli and Neely 2010; Audit Commission and I&DeA 2002)—tend to pull the focus away from systemic approaches to improvement. Approaches clustered under New Public Governance (Osborne 2006, 2010) are also influential here. In addition, a focus on continuous improvement makes a stronger claim to having been generally a positive force, and benchmarking (Magd and Curry 2003) allows learning from historical comparative performance to inform future performance, as was the intention with the Beacon Council scheme (Rashman and Radnor 2005).

Mode Four: Service Design (Individual and Prospective)

Finally, mode four embraces a domain of activity that has been the subject of significant recent discussion—the 'co-production' of value (Osborne et al. 2016). This happens through adopting and adapting consumer- or user-driven approaches to developing and improving services, as well as efforts to democratise individual funding decisions such as participatory budgeting or the move towards enabling social care to be delivered via individual budgets rather than organisationally specified care packages. Here, we see efforts to set the optimal conditions for future accountability through enabling service design and involving users or consumers of services more deeply, and in the future design of services. The move towards enshrining user values, perspectives, and needs in service design, as well as service delivery, goes some way towards addressing historical concerns about the inflexibility or paternalistic approach to services that emerged through the Public Administration perspective (Osborne and Strokosch 2013).

Figure 2.1 places effective accountability at the centre of the two sets of tensions that we have outlined in the evaluative model.

The four modes outlined here are not simply taxonomical, but to allow a more nuanced unpacking of differing approaches to, and understanding of, accountability. Broadly, we argue for the need to better understand whether we are attempting to *build in* accountability through establishing the future circumstances needed, or whether the focus should be on identifying significant underperformance or failures in delivery; what we might call a deficit model of accountability. Clearly,

Tensions in public assurance

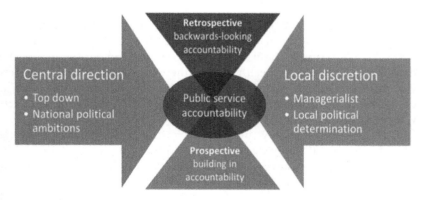

Fig. 2.1   Public service accountability tensions

effective public service accountability must draw upon both of these broad approaches, and indeed may require all four of the modes we have articulated above.

However, we make two further points. Firstly, in alignment with the concepts underpinning the 'strategy as practice' literature (Whittington 1996; Hodgkinson and Hughes 2014), we do not wish to suggest that our model is normative. Rather, we have developed a model based on the research that informs the following empirical chapters and additional investigations. Our evaluative model aims to further the discussion around how multiple and sometimes competing forms of accountability may be analysed, critiqued, and developed, drawing out theoretical positions from the reality of accountability as practised.

Secondly, too often local service institutions are discussed as if they were homogenous blocks, and this risks eliding the subtleties of local service discretion as valid local political choices. Local political determination is an essential component of local government, and we expect to be able to hold our local politicians to account at the ballot box for their achievements, choices, or failures. The increasing politicisation of fire and rescue and police services would appear to address the perceptions of a democratic deficit in those services, but this is not enough alone. This book argues that democratic accountability is only one of the existing types, and is necessary, but alone is insufficient to facilitate strong public *service* accountability.

CONCLUSION

We have deliberately avoided making value judgements based on comparative analyses between the sectors. Health and social care are not 'worse' at delivering accountability than local government because of the democratic deficit in the health service; these are merely facets of the service delivery context. Additionally, a divergence exists between different police forces or different councils, as well as within individual local service institutions.

Effective accountability must, therefore, embrace the competing tensions within and between service institutions and adapt to the necessary granularity required; accountability mechanisms must be contingent if they are to be effective. This sense of contingency should also be based on a pragmatic understanding of the other forces arrayed: that is the quality of political and managerial leadership; the current appetite for embracing new forms of managing services and holding them to account; the quality of systems, processes, and competencies in managing the multiple forms of accountability; and the demographic, financial, and service demand challenges facing the individual organisations.

This now leads to a question: If we cannot clearly say what is the 'best' or 'right' model of accountability, how should we approach making improvements in the effectiveness of accountability processes? Whilst the specific configuration of accountability modes is rightly a matter for the service, organisation, or sector to address rather than for us to impose, we believe a series of design principlesfor effective accountability which can be articulated to help develop the most effective approach.

This chapter, therefore, concludes by raising some of the design principles for effective accountability identified so far that arise from the evaluative model. Primarily, we propose that effective accountability is developed through a consideration of:

- Balancing forward-looking and backward-looking forms
- Negotiating the tensions between centrally imposed and locally determined (and individual and systemic forms)
- The integration of financial and performance accountability along with quantitative and qualitative methods

The following empirical chapters will develop these themes, having further established the principles from the practices observed and evaluated, before the final chapter returns to this theme by coalescing a final set of propositions for designing accountability into effective public service delivery.

REFERENCES

Ahrens, T., & Ferry, L. (2015). Newcastle City Council and the Grassroots: Accountability and Budgeting Under Austerity. *Accounting, Auditing & Accountability Journal, 28*(6), 909–933.

Audit Commission, I&DeA. (2002). *Acting on Facts: Using Performance Measurement to Improve Local Authority Services*. London: Audit Commission.

Bevan, G., & Hood, C. (2006). What's Measured Is What Matters: Targets and Gaming in the English Public Health Care System. *Public Administration, 84*(3), 517–538.

Bovens, M., Schillemans, T., & Goodin, R. E. (2014). Public Accountability. In M. Bovens, R. E. Goodin, & T. Schillemans (Eds.), *The Oxford Handbook of Public Accountability* (pp. 1–22). Oxford: Oxford University Press.

Chandler, J. A. (Ed.). (2000). *Comparative Public Administration*. London: Routledge.

Committee on Standards in Public Life. (1995). *Standards in Public Life: First Report of the Committee on Standards in Public Life*. London.

DCLG. (2011a). *Armchair Auditors Are Here to Stay*. London: HMG.

DCLG. (2011b). Localism Act (2011), c.20. London: HMSO.

Denhardt, J. V., & Denhardt, R. B. (2015). *The New Public Service: Serving, Not Steering* (4th ed.). Abingdon: Routledge.

Dewar, D., & Funnell, W. (2017). *A History of British National Audit: The Pursuit of Accountability*. Oxford: Oxford University Press.

DTLR. (2000). Local Government Act 2000. Vol c.22. London: TSO.

Dubnick, M. J. (2014). Accountability as a Cultural Keyword. In M. Bovens, R. E. Goodin, & T. Schillemans (Eds.), *The Oxford Handbook of Public Accountability* (pp. 23–38). Oxford: Oxford University Press.

Eckersley, P., Ferry, L., & Zakaria, Z. (2014). A 'Panoptical' or 'Synoptical' Approach to Monitoring Performance? Local Public Services in England and the Widening Accountability Gap. *Critical Perspectives on Accounting, 25*(6), 529–538.

Ferry, L., Eckersley, P., & Zakaria, Z. (2015). Accountability and Transparency in English Local Government: Moving from 'Matching Parts' to 'Awkward Couple'? *Financial Accountability & Management, 31*(3), 345–361.

Ferry, L., & Murphy, P. (2015). *Financial Sustainability, Accountability and Transparency Across Local Public Service Bodies in England Under Austerity* (Report to National Audit Office (NAO)). London: National Audit Office.

Foucault, M. (1977). *Discipline and Punish* (A. Sheridan, Trans.). New York: Pantheon.

Foucault, M. (1991). *The Foucault Reader*, Rabinow, P. (Ed.). London: Penguin Books Ltd.

Gray, A., & Jenkins, B. (1993). Codes of Accountability in the New Public Sector. *Accounting, Auditing & Accountability Journal, 6*(3). 52–67

Gray, A., & Jenkins, B. (1995). From Public Administration to Public Management: Reassessing A Revolution? *Public Administration, 73*(1), 75–99.

Hodgkinson, I., & Hughes, P. (2014). Strategy Content and Public Service Provider Performance in the UK: An Alternative Approach. *Public Administration, 92*(3), 707–726.

Home Office. (2017). Policing and Crime Act 2017. c.3.

Hood, C. (2006). Gaming in Targetworld: The Targets Approach to Managing British Public Services. *Public Administration Review, 66*(4), 515–521.

Hood, C. (2007). Public Service Management by Numbers: Why Does It Vary? Where Has It Come from? What Are the Gaps and the Puzzles? *Public Money and Management, 27*(2), 95–102.

Hood, C. (2010). Accountability and Transparency: Siamese Twins, Matching Parts, Awkward Couple? *West European Politics, 33*(5), 989–1009.

Magd, H., & Curry, A. (2003). Benchmarking: Achieving Best Value in Public-Sector Organisations. *Benchmarking: An International Journal, 10*(3), 261–286.

Micheli, P., & Neely, A. (2010). Performance Measurement in the Public Sector in England: Searching for the Golden Thread. *Public Administration Review, 70*(4), 591–600.

Moynihan, D. P., & Pandey, S. K. (2007). The Role of Organizations in Fostering Public Service Motivation. *Public Administration Review, 67*(1), 40–53.

Normann, R. (2000). *Service Management: Strategy and Leadership in Service Business* (3rd ed.). Chichester: Wiley.

Osborne, S. P. (2006). The New Public Governance? *Public Management Review, 8*(3), 377–387.

Osborne, S. P. (Ed.). (2010). *The New Public Governance? Emerging Perspectives on the Theory and Practice of Public Governance.* Abingdon: Routledge.

Osborne, S. P., Radnor, Z., & Strokosch, K. (2016). Co-production and the Co-creation of Value in Public Services: A Suitable Case for Treatment? *Public Management Review, 18*(5), 639–653.

Osborne, S. P., & Strokosch, K. (2013). It Takes Two to Tango? Understanding the Co-production of Public Services by Integrating the Services Management and Public Administration Perspectives. *British Journal of Management, 24*, S31–S47.

Perry, J. L., & Wise, L. R. (1990). The Motivational Bases of Public Service. *Public Administration Review, 50*(3), 367.

Radnor, Z. (2011). Hitting the Target and Missing the Point? Developing an Understanding of Organizational Gaming. In W. Van Dooren & S. Van de Walle (Eds.), *Performance Information in the Public Sector: How It Is Used* (pp. 98–109). Basingstoke: Palgrave Macmillan.

Rashman, L., & Radnor, Z. (2005). Learning to Improve: Approaches to Improving Local Government Services. *Public Money & Management, 25*(1), 19–26.

Stewart, J. (2000). *The Nature of British Local Government.* Basingstoke: Government Beyond the Centre—Macmillan Press.

Svara, J. H. (2008). Beyond Dichotomy: Dwight Waldo and the Intertwined Politics-Administration Relationship. *Public Administration Review, 68*(1), 46–52.

Warren, M. E. (2014). Accountability and Democracy. In M. Bovens, R. E. Goodin, & T. Schillemans (Eds.), *The Oxford Handbook of Public Accountability* (pp. 39–54). Oxford: Oxford University Press.

Whittington, R. (1996). Strategy as Practice. *Long Range Planning, 29*(5), 731–735.

CHAPTER 3

Local Government

Laurence Ferry, Russ Glennon and Peter Murphy

Abstract This is the first of four chapters that investigate each of the service areas that were the responsibility of the former Audit Commission. Local Government is the most obviously accountable public service because of the direct democratic interface between citizens and the governing mechanisms. It also has the most diverse and complex accountability arrangements. In this chapter, we distinguish between the period of the coalition government and that of the minority Conservative administration. We illustrate the development, or in the case of local government, the significant weakening of the regime between 2010 and 2015 by using the previous model and we use the new model for evaluating the changes in the regime since 2015.

Keywords Local government · Accountability · Transparency · Public assurance

INTRODUCTION

Under the New Labour administrations of 1997–2010, and before the financial crisis of 2008 onwards, local government was at the forefront of development in accountability and performance management regimes with different sectoral and/or service regimes mutually learning from their own and each other's experiences. It is argued that the 'regimes' tended towards coalescence (Murphy 2014), rather than diversification

© The Author(s) 2019   47
P. Murphy et al., *Public Service Accountability*,
https://doi.org/10.1007/978-3-319-93384-9_3

although some disagree (Goldfinch and Wallis 2010). It has also been suggested that such regimes had a significant impact in Europe, Australia, Canada and, to a lesser extent, the USA (Christensen and Laegreid 2011).

However, since 2010 and the policy of 'austerity-localism' (Lowndes and Pratchett 2012) local authorities were given more powers over their activities, but also endured some of the largest budgets cuts of any public services and far in excess of the levels of reduction in central government expenditure (HM Treasury 2010).

In a period of austerity, it might be reasonable to expect 'value for money' from more limited resources to be an even greater priority than it was before. Austerity challenged the financial sustainability of local governments and the ability of policymakers to address policy challenges. Having appropriate accountability and transparency arrangements to assure the public they were getting value for money should have taken on renewed urgency. However, contrary to this, the period of the coalition government saw the dismantling of and disinvestment in the 'improvement infrastructure' and the data and intelligence that had formed the evidence base for the reform and improvement of local authority services.

The purpose of this chapter is to consider the financial and service sustainability of local government under the Conservative-led coalition government from 2010 to 2015. The accountability, transparency, and public assurance arrangements will be evaluated via the concepts identified as part of the evaluative framework in Chapter 2.

CENTRAL AND LOCAL GOVERNMENT RELATIONSHIPS

The size and sustained nature of the public spending cuts led to fears around both the financial and service sustainability of public services. Any reform to state institutions by politicians and public managers has to consider the relationship between central government, local government, and citizens, particularly given the significant influence on policy-making (Moynihan 2008).

More specifically, literature has highlighted challenges of implementation around performance management in the public sector (Van Dooren et al. 2015), particularly at sub-national tiers of government (Ashworth et al. 2007), identifying tensions between central control and local determination.

Since the 1980s, successive governments employed national performance management frameworksaccumulating information about how sub-national levels of government are operating, more than at any point historically. However, the emphasis of government on some performance management aspects, such as building measurement systems to acquire more performance data, was not always matched by wider organisational change initiatives to facilitate using the information at the level of implementation (Van Dooren et al. 2015; Moynihan 2008).

In the UK context, power and control in central and local government relations have been continually contested, especially around service determination, performance management and funding arrangements (Rhodes 1981; Wilson and Game 2011). Since the early 1990s, there has been a gradual centralisation of funding following the poll tax (a local tax based on housing prices) being axed. Indeed, arguably, England of all major Western European countries has the most central control over local government funds (Ferry et al. 2015a).

From the early 1980s, UK governments of all political persuasions have also supplemented financial controls with an increasing range of centralised performance management frameworks setting out local government scope and operations in detail (Seal and Ball 2005, 2011; Seal 2003). A 'golden thread' was to be created linking ministerial objectives and pronouncements with the administration of policy at the local level (Micheli and Neely 2010). Individual local authority performance could then be monitored against these frameworks through a comprehensive system of indicators and external audit and inspection, and ultimately ranked in league tables encouraging comparative benchmarking and competition. The underlying aim of these initiatives was continuous improvement in public services. Continuous improvement was to be assessed through the 3Es, i.e. economy, efficiency, and effectiveness—value for money—with which local authorities delivered the services that were reflected in national indicators and performance frameworks (Hopwood 1984).

In contrast to developments since the 1980s, from 2010 the Conservative-led coalition government embraced 'austerity localism' as an overriding policy objective (Lowndes and Pratchett 2012) and began systematic and systemic governing and budgeting for deficit reduction through radical changes to the spending review, budget, and audit and accountability arrangements (Ferry and Eckersley 2011, 2012, 2015b). *The Localism Act 2011* did not, however, give local authorities greater autonomy over local revenue generation to go with the increased power they were perceived to have over spending decisions. Abandonment of performance management frameworks and performance audit has meant less focus from local authorities on service outputs and outcomes (NAO 2014a). Other changes included the abolition of the Audit Commission that had co-ordinated and delivered external audit, inspection and national reporting on locally delivered public services in the UK (Timmins and Gash 2014).

It was also determined that future local authority audits would be overseen centrally by the NAO, would focus solely on financial management, and have no performance assessment in the *Local Audit and Accountability Act 2014* (Ellwood 2014). This, coupled with austerity, made *'financial conformance'* not *'operational performance'* the overriding focus, for both central and local government (NAO 2014b) weakening local accountability by obscuring austerity cuts in terms of their potential impacts, especially on value for money (Ferry and Eckersley 2015b).

Unfortunately, the changes in public service provision have increased the risk of provider failure (National Audit Office 2014a) and performance at an *individual* local authority level had an accountability deficit that is only partially addressed through the NAO report on financial sustainability (NAO 2014a). Assessing the value for money aspects of financial sustainability became a challenge due to the lack or inadequacy of performance information available. Unlike the Audit Commission's much wider remit, the NAO's obligation was essentially reduced to highlighting risks that certain local authorities may not be able to set a balanced budget or fulfil statutory duties. The key messages of its 2014 local government report were:

> There is little evidence of the extent to which local authorities have made savings through efficiencies rather than service reductions. Other than data on children's and adult social care, there are almost no data on local authority outputs and activities. Assessing how far savings have impacted on service users for most service areas, based on comparable national data is not possible for the most part. (NAO 2014a)

Essentially, the NAO commentary identified that the new accountability and audit arrangements could show if the DCLG and local authorities were spending within budget, but not what value for money the public was receiving.

More broadly, delivery mechanism diversification encouraged by the coalition government has created a much more complex accountability landscape (Shaoul et al. 2012). This, coupled with local authorities recognising that their traditional organisational remit and funding arrangements would have to change further, altered the local government risk profile (Ferry et al. 2017). Figure 3.1 illustrates the change between 2010 and 2015.

In an attempt to mitigate the reduction in accountability arrangements, there were repeated claims by ministers that the transparency agenda would lead to an army of 'armchair auditors' that would fill the accountability void created by the closure of the Audit Commission and the abandonment of performance audit (DCLG 2011a), but this did not materialise. As a result, the quality of service outputs and outcomes were not being comprehensively or robustly assessed (Ferry et al. 2015b). When combined with austerity, this reinforced the holding down of input costs through an overriding focus on budgetary stewardship as the pre-dominant managerial objective within local authorities, and meant a reduced scope for officers to innovate (Ferry et al. 2015b). The transparency agenda in England is arguably an apologia and not an effective substitute for the level and sophistication of accountability that can be afforded by independent professional auditors assessing performance (Ferry et al. 2015b). However, internationally this is not always the case as context, culture and politics can play a role alongside other contingent variables (Ferry et al. 2015b; Ospina et al. 2004; Willems and Van Dooren 2012; Molnár 2008).

The idea of the public as armchair auditors may not have taken hold (Ferry and Eckersley 2015a; Etzioni 2014) but, nevertheless, social movements, political protests, citizen participation and other bottom-up grassroots initiatives did influence policy contestation (Ball and Seal 2005) and led to various governance changes, co-option strategies, challenges to government policy from the local level (Ahrens and Ferry 2018), public value accounting strategies, and hybridisation of financial and service roles (Ahrens et al. 2018).

In England, between 2010 and 2015, accountability arrangements diminished and were not adequately replaced by transparency initiatives. Nonetheless, international experience suggests that over the longer-term,

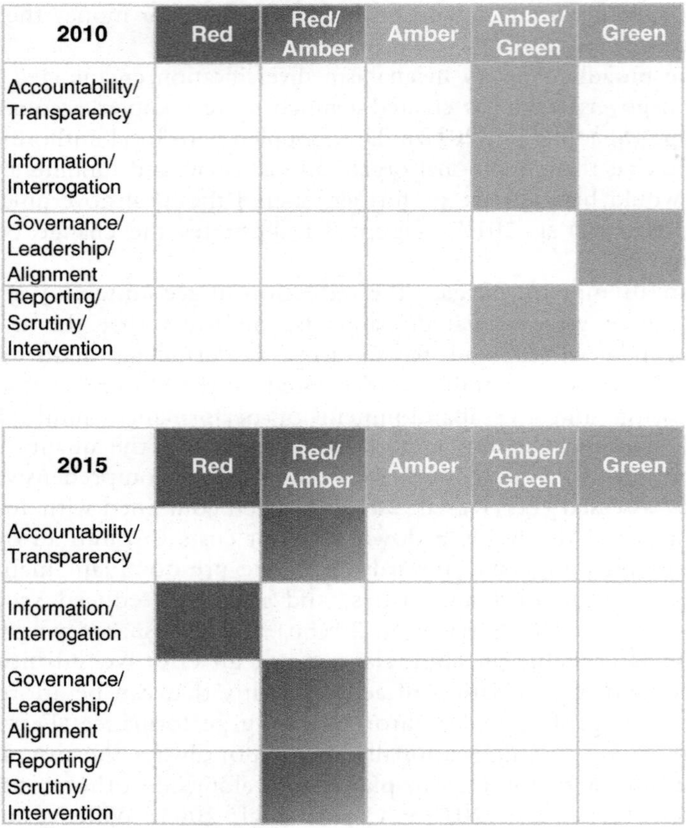

2010	Red	Red/ Amber	Amber	Amber/ Green	Green
Accountability/ Transparency				▓	
Information/ Interrogation				▓	
Governance/ Leadership/ Alignment					▓
Reporting/ Scrutiny/ Intervention				▓	

2015	Red	Red/ Amber	Amber	Amber/ Green	Green
Accountability/ Transparency		▓			
Information/ Interrogation	▓				
Governance/ Leadership/ Alignment		▓			
Reporting/ Scrutiny/ Intervention		▓			

Fig. 3.1   Local Government: Public Assurance 2010–2015

some performance information use will be re-introduced as financial stress eases and there is a focus once again on value for money, and not merely cutback management (Raudla et al. 2013; Wildavsky 1975). As a result, it is important to consider a number of themes in the light of critical reflection by academics, policymakers, and practitioners. These contribute to a broader debate on accountability and transparency as they are particularly important pillars underpinning our democratic system of governance. They are also important to jurisdictions with other forms of governance. We consider five themes, which will be followed by some general conclusions based on our evaluative framework.

CAN TRANSPARENCY ADEQUATELY REPLACE ACCOUNTABILITY?

Local government in England was, by 2015, in a more complex organisational landscape where accountability had been reduced and not adequately replaced by increased transparency. For example, in terms of accountability, the focus is primarily on financial conformance and sector-led improvement (SLI) by local government itself (House of Commons Communities and Local Government Committee 2011). The abolition of the Audit Commission and decommissioning of corporate performance management arrangements have meant that value for money capability and capacity has been significantly reduced. Policymakers must, therefore, decide if they need to strengthen accountability. This will become paramount when austerity as an overarching policy recedes and the focus on cutback management gives way to a revived interest in value for money.

Local authorities are established in statute, with a responsibility to their electorate for spending decisions and have responsibilities mainly covered by a framework of legal duties which set out what they must do and places checks and balances on their actions. These duties include the role of officers and councillors and accountability to the public.

Local authorities are also subject to strict financial controls, including having a balanced budget for revenue and expenditure. The principal local checks that are made on regularity and propriety cover clarity in terms of responsibility for resources, a set of financial duties and rules requiring prudence in spending, internal checks that rules are followed, and external checks by an independent auditor.

Audit arrangements are subject to the Local Audit and Accountability Act 2014. This repealed the Audit Commission Act 1998 and reformed processes for performance and financial audit of local government. These reforms included the abolition of the Audit Commission which closed on 31st March 2015 and transferred a number of its responsibilities to other organisations, including the NAO. In place of the Audit Commission, there is a new framework for local public audit that started after the Commission's current contracts with audit suppliers ended in 2016/2017. A transitional body, Public Sector Audit Appointments

Limited (PSAA), now oversees the contracts in the period up to 2022/2233. The NAO produces the code of practice and supporting guidelines for local authorities, as well as enhancing its existing value for money studies by conducting a small number of investigations into local public service delivery.

The audit changes require local authorities to adjust to dealing with relatively more organisations. These include the PSAA, NAO, Cabinet Office and the Department for Communities and Local Government (DCLG). Local authorities also liaise with government departments, regulators and auditors about various issues previously dealt with or coordinated by the Audit Commission. *The Local Audit and Accountability Act 2014* does not provide for national collation and reporting of local audit results, although PSAA will publish information on results of auditors' work with local government bodies until current contracts end. After that, there is no clear or specific commitment to producing reports setting out the big picture across local government or health services.

In short, the new local audit arrangements break up the old regulatory framework. The NAO, Financial Reporting Council, recognised supervisory bodies, local auditor panels and audit firms all have parts to play in the new landscape. This creates uncertainties about how local appointment and oversight of auditors will work.

In terms of performance management, the coalition government dismantled much of the performance management framework for local government, replacing centrally driven performance reporting and data requirements with sector self-regulation, transparency and local accountability. Following the abolition of national performance frameworks, local authorities and the LGA introduced an SLI approach to improvement (House of Commons 2011; Local Government Association 2011; Timmins and Gash 2014). This was based on four underlying principles: local authorities are responsible for their own performance; local authorities should be accountable locally not nationally; there is a sense of collective responsibility for the performance of the sector as a whole; the role of the LGA is to provide tools and support (LGA 2011, 2014, 2015).

The LGA provided practical support to help local authorities make the most of the opportunities afforded by this improvement approach. This included support of a corporate nature such as leadership programmes, peer challenge and a benchmarking service (LG Inform), plus programmes tailored to specific sectors—such as children's and adults' services, health, financial, culture, tourism, sport and planning services. In terms of transparency, *the Local Authority (Executive Arrangements) (Meetings and Access to Information) (England) Regulations 2012* introduced marginally greater transparency and access to local authority meetings. The *Local Government Transparency Code*, updated twice since its introduction (DCLG 2015b), lists a range of datasets that local authorities must make available to the public. These include publication of annual accounts and each line of spending worth over £500. It also comprises senior employee salaries, councillor allowances and expenses, copies of contracts and tenders, and grants to the voluntary and social enterprise sectors. Furthermore, it includes policies, performance and external audit, and key inspections, although there are no longer any external corporate inspections.

INFORMAL OR AMATEUR AUDITING ARRANGEMENTS

There has been a significant loss of capacity and capability concerning information and its interrogation, which is partially due to the Audit Commission's abolition and the subsequent dismantling of performance management arrangements.

As previously mentioned, the army of 'armchair auditors' envisioned by the government has not materialised to fill the accountability deficit (Ferry and Eckersley 2015b). This created significant challenges for practitioners in being able to ascertain what programmes to undertake and in determining which of those may provide value for money. The evidence base is diminished and so decisions become more open to opinion and political choice. A diverse range of information may be used by citizens to make a judgment (that is, if they bother) and there is relatively less independent evidence to refute or support such judgments.

The investigation and analysis of expenditure and performance information is still possible through DCLG's local authority statistics and CIPFA's financial and performance databases, although the latter is a subscriber-only service. Having said that, the collection, analysis, availability, transparency and interrogation of these data and other local authority statistics has become increasingly difficult since 2010. Primarily, this is due to the Audit Commission's operational research and evaluation capacity no longer existing. For example, numerous reports on local government, value for money, and improvement were produced by the Audit

Commission between 1983 and 2010, with a more limited range between 2010 and 2015. As well as the abolition of the Audit Commission, the earlier closure of the 'Improvement and Development Agency (I&DeA)' for local government also constrained capacity and capability. In addition, the DCLG's internal research and evaluation capacity underwent a significant reduction, as did some of the external bodies. Even if this army of armchair auditors emerged, they would find it very difficult to draw meaningful conclusions and recommendations from the available raw data (House of Commons Public Accounts Committee 2015).

The development of operational research capacity and capability at the NAO has only partially compensated for the loss of capacity that previously existed across the other bodies. Historically there has been some independent academic research capacity in the management of local authorities, but as evidenced in the proceedings and minutes of the Public Administration Committee of the Joint Universities Council, academic research and teaching of public management in general has significantly declined over this period as reductions in public expenditure and increases in tuition fees in England have affected enrolments.

AUSTERITY AND CUTBACK MANAGEMENT

The theory and practice of cutback management were adopted during the sustained period of austerity in England. This coupled with localism for English local government (Lowndes and Pratchett 2012) has challenged practitioners in the governance of their local authorities, the leadership of services, and strategic alignment of plans and delivery, especially those involving multiple partners. Practitioners must understand the pressures and risks associated with cutback management, but also make provision for governance, leadership and strategic alignment concerning the future when austerity recedes and value for money re-emerges.

CIPFA and the Society of Local Authority Chief Executives (SOLACE) issued *Delivering Good Governance in Local Government: Framework and Accompanying Guidance Note* in 2007, which was updated in 2012 through an addendum and revisions to assist in good governance. This is important as maintaining and improving governance is a key responsibility of the council leader and head of paid service (chief executive officer or equivalent). There are also designated statutory roles and responsibilities for a local authority's chief executive officer, chief financial officer and the monitoring officer. The local authority is legally obliged to maintain a balanced budget and the chief financial officer discharges this statutory function. Additionally, statutory requirements are associated with the roles and responsibilities of the director of children's services and the director of adult services. There is also a responsibility on all members of the leadership team, full council or authority, and those responsible for monitoring and providing assurance on governance arrangements for ensuring strategic alignment.

With regard to strategic alignment, DCLG awarded the CIPFA/SOLACE framework 'proper practices' status through non-statutory guidance. As a result, local authorities have to prepare and publish an annual governance statement that accompanies the statement of accounts to meet a statutory requirement set out in Regulation 4(2) of the *Accounts and Audit Regulations 2003*, as amended by the *Accounts and Audit (Amendment) (England) Regulations 2006*. This regulation requires local authorities to prepare a statement of internal control in accordance with the framework's 'proper practices' for developing and maintaining a local code of governance and for discharging accountability for the proper conduct of public business. These statements follow a standardised template set out in the framework, whereby local authorities make their practices and structures open and explicit, mapping them against agreed best practices. This helps ensure strategic alignment of governance practices.

Good governance and strategic alignment enable a local authority's leadership to pursue its vision effectively and also underpins that vision with control and the management of risk. However, strategic alignment is under pressure as local government has been undergoing significant change in an increasingly complex environment of austerity localism. In addition to economic and financial sustainability challenges, the *Localism Act 2011* and other legislation have brought new roles, opportunities and greater flexibility. Local authorities have been changing their models of service delivery for some time (Alford and O'Flynn 2012); local public services are now delivered directly through partnerships, collaboration, commissioning, outsourcing, local authority trading companies and by combined authorities. Strategic alignment is challenged by the introduction of these new structures and ways of working in terms of managing risk, ensuring transparency, and demonstrating accountability (Shaoul et al. 2012).

CONSTRAINED PUBLIC REPORTING, SCRUTINY, AND PUBLIC ASSURANCE

Public assurance of value for money became more difficult to establish due to the changes to performance management information that have meant reporting is more partial, scrutiny has become more variable, structures have changed, and quality assurance is receding with the demise of the professionalised performance audit. Intervention is still available via sector-led improvement (Bennett et al. 2014), but practitioners are implicitly expected to ensure arrangements are in place for mitigating shortfalls in reporting and scrutiny, and for working with the wider local government community in support of the SLI regime.

Financial information is now the sole focus of local authority financial reporting to central government. The reports are based on the statutory requirement for local authorities to ensure accountability and transparency for financial stewardship, which is set out in the *Local Government Act 1972*. A single individual, the Section 151 Officer (who is often the finance director, and must be a qualified accountant), is personally responsible for producing a balanced revenue budget every year. The *Local Government Act 2003*makes a balanced budget a requirement and the Section 151 officer has to report on the robustness of estimates and adequacy of reserves. These budgets and reports are then subject to a financial audit.

The statutory requirement for local authorities to produce performance reports for central government has not existed since 2010, although for local accountability purposes a small and diminishing minority of authorities still publish them. In addition, other central government departments sometimes attach specific conditions to individual funding streams or grants requiring local authorities to report how the money was spent.

The *Local Government Act 2000*established internal 'overview and scrutiny' committees as a counterbalance to the new executive structures created by that Act that required all large local authorities to introduce either elected mayors or a leader and cabinet system. The role of these committees was to develop and review policy and make recommendations to the council. Following the Localism Act 2011, councils with executive governance arrangements are only required to have one overview and scrutiny committee that is independent of the executive. The Act also permitted councils to revert to the previous committee system if they wanted—in which case they can operate overview and scrutiny committees if they so wish, but are not required to.

Working with other local public services through inter-agency and collaborative arrangements is also 'horizontally' scrutinised to a degree in local resilience forums, health and wellbeing boards and community safety partnerships. Services can also use CIPFA's interactive financial database and interrogative tools to benchmark with other bodies, regarding expenditure and budgeting.

Local authorities also manage processes of 'external scrutiny' through their committees looking at issues that lie outside the council's direct responsibilities. For example, specific powers exist to scrutinise health bodies, crime and disorder partnerships, Police and Crime Commissioners, and flood risk management authorities. In the context of growing multiple collaborative arrangements and proposals for further devolution of powers to local government, the Centre for Public Scrutiny proposed the creation of local public accounts committees to scrutinise the whole range of public spending within a given area (Centre for Public Scrutiny 2018) so this scrutiny gap can be addressed.

The Department of Health has prepared guidance to help local government and their partners in scrutinising public health services more effectively. However, because local authorities either commission or provide public health services of their own, as well as commission or provide health services for the National Health Service (NHS), they are themselves within the scope of health scrutiny legislation. In other words, local authorities may be both a scrutineer and scrutinee of health services.

In many local authorities, the overview and scrutiny committees have separate staff and financial resources. However, annual surveys conducted by the Centre for Public Scrutiny indicate constantly diminishing resources over the last eight years (Centre for Public Scrutiny 2015). A call has been made from the centre for local authorities to 'up their game' concerning scrutiny following the scandal associated with children's services in Rotherham (Centre for Public Scrutiny 2014), and a recent report highlighting concerns from officers and councillors that they no longer provide sufficient interrogation and scrutiny (Grant Thornton 2015).

Ultimately, the political leadership of local authorities that fail to deliver for their local communities can be voted out by their electorate. However, there are also external systems in place for intervention should they fail to fulfil their functions regarding maintenance of regularity, propriety and value for money. In cases affecting an individual, for example, the Local Government Ombudsman provides an independent route of complaint and redress. For service specific failure, such as in children's services, the relevant government department has in some cases put in place specific failure and improvement regimes. In terms of the overall corporate performance of a local authority, the LGA coordinates the local government sector in providing peer support to local authorities (LGA 2014). As a last resort, central government through the *Local Government Acts 1999* and *2003* still has powers to investigate and intervene.

A systematic approach has been put in place by the LGA to identify local authorities where 'preventative improvement support' could benefit them. To do so, the approach is based on published financial and service delivery data from inspectorates and regulators, data and informal information from peer challenge, and 'informal conversations' with the sector (LGA 2014). Information sharing arrangements are in place between the LGA and government departments and the Inspectorates to ensure the LGA has the intelligence to focus support. Alongside this, the DCLG and local government's 'localities' arrangements—where all the senior civil servants in the department are twinned with one or more local authorities—offer senior-level engagement with each local authority area. This is separate from performance considerations focusing mainly on policy and implementation, although information is shared where appropriate. These arrangements replaced the much more comprehensive network of government regional offices, which were also abolished in 2011 by the coalition government (DCLG 2010).

The LGA can initiate a SLI process when an issue is identified. If a resolution cannot be found for the issue, or if there is a refusal from the local authority to engage with the improvement process, the Secretary of State can seek to ensure a robust evidence base through commissioning a corporate governance investigation. The personal authority to do this follows on from the Local Government Act 1999 and the Local Audit and Accountability Act 2014, which abolished the Audit Commission. These acts also give the Secretary of State the power to direct local authorities to take actions, and ultimately to direct another body to take over specific functions of a local authority, if the authority is unwilling to engage with the LGA in light of the evidence gathered after an investigation.

Following the government's experience of intervention in Doncaster (Le Grand et al. 2013), the DCLG developed a model for handling future interventions, which involved working closely with the local government sector. It is debatable whether SLI has been, or will be, more effective than central intervention, although even its strongest proponents in the LGA accept the latter must remain an option to incentivise local authorities to engage with the SLI and provide a fall-back position if the SLI proves insufficient (Bennett et al. 2014; Murphy and Jones 2016).

PLACING VALUE FOR MONEY AT RISK

As a consequence of the challenges of austerity localism, real potential value for money risks have surfaced for the financial sustainability and resilience of local government, coupled with significant changes to accountability and transparency arrangements. For instance, central control over local government revenue (grants, business rates, and council tax) means an individual local authority has very limited ability to adapt to sudden increases in demand, plan robustly, or fill growing resource gaps. The introduction of indicative three-year funding agreements only mitigates the risks to a small extent providing some room for identifying where pressures may be absorbed, and a local authority's ability to raise revenue through fees and charges or other sources of income is also limited to addressing problems at the margins. The NAO's key findings noted that:

> Some local authorities are showing persistent signs of fiscal stress particularly metropolitan districts…[that]…local auditors' confidence that local authorities can make medium-term savings has fallen…[and that]…auditors are concerned about 'funding gaps' within local authorities medium-term plans, and the risks that could prevent authorities delivering savings. (NAO 2014b)

The *Local Audit and Accountability Act 2014* statutory requirements concentrate on annual financial reporting, which may hinder broader short, medium and long-term sustainable management of financial and other resources. Other parts of the performance management and/or public assurance regimes do not mitigate these risks, which could be perceived as a weakness of the current regime over previous performance and financial assurance arrangements.

Overall, then, the problem is compounded by the dismantling of centralised performance monitoring frameworks, comparable quality assured indicators and the abolition of the Audit Commission itself. This ultimately means that there is insufficient data available on the quality and scope of local government services, as well as very limited capacity and capability to interrogate this data effectively. This obscures any risks associated with service performance, and means an informed judgment on a local authority's value for money is all but impossible. Armchair auditors have not stepped into the breach to mitigate this risk, and the NAO is limited to undertaking high-level assessments of value for money across the sector, rather than within individual local authorities.

EVALUATION OF ACCOUNTABILITY

Local government is often considered the most obviously accountable public service because of the direct democratic interface that exists between citizens and the governing mechanisms. This is why there is a more significant body of research and writing on local government, and why it features strongly in the Public Administration and New Public Management literature.

English local government encompasses (at the last count) some 650+ individual services, and quite a few of these operate in a fashion that is amenable to classical (private sector) managerialist philosophy, i.e. managed largely by focusing on interactions between consumer and service provider. As we have argued, this is appropriate for many services, and forms mode one of our four-mode model of accountability. Service management and satisfaction surveys are appropriate tools for managing a range of public services such as, say, libraries, or leisure services where direct comparison and competitors exist (Hodgkinson et al. 2017).

The focus of this chapter, and indeed this book, has not been on the traditional democratic accountability processes; those are more than adequately covered elsewhere (see, for example Behn 2001; Gray and Jenkins 1993; Mulgan 2000; Svara 2001; Warren 2014). Our focus is on the understanding of what makes *public service accountability* a distinctive lens through which to understand English local government and beyond.

Our evaluative model provides a new perspective on the wide range of mechanisms imposed on, or 'suggested' to, local government. The wide range of services, the presence of direct democratic mechanisms, and the long history of local government reform have all contributed to a complex set of accountability arrangements.

And yet, the New Labour administrations made significant use of accountability mechanisms through the second mode—institutional comparisons—via overarching performance management frameworks including *Best Value* and associated performance indicators (DETR 1999; DTLR 2000), and institutional assessments such as *Comprehensive Performance Assessment* (CPA) (Audit Commission 2002, 2005; DTLR 2001) and *Comprehensive Area Assessment* (CAA) (Audit Commission 2009; Department of Communities and Local Government 2007). These institutional comparisons provided a limited but universal method of highlighting service performance between authorities, further enhanced by the use of statistical 'nearest neighbours' tools to optimise the appropriateness of comparisons.

This regulatory environment was accompanied by a push towards comparison and learning approaches, such as *Beacon Councils* (Rashman and Radnor 2005) or more general benchmarking (Magd and Curry 2003). Much of this overall reform trajectory was badged under the local government 'modernisation' agenda (Glennon et al. 2018). This modernisation agenda encompassed both service and democratic reforms.

Local government has a statutory *Best Value* duty, introduced in 2000 and reconfirmed in 2015, which requires it to 'make arrangements to secure continuous improvement in the way in which its functions are exercised, having regard to a combination of economy, efficiency, and effectiveness' (Department of Communities and Local Government 2015a). This puts a clear emphasis on mode three, accountability as a mechanism for facilitating continuous improvement, with an emphasis on prospective assurance. However, the 2011 guidance also states in the foreword by Eric Pickles:

Local councils have been freed from excessive and prescriptive guidance and duties in return for a 'social responsibility' deal which asks that they continue to give support to local voluntary and community groups and small businesses. (Department of Communities and Local Government 2011b)

Here, we see efforts to place local government in the fourth mode of service design—a loosening of 'red tape' to be accompanied by a more pluralistic role for the community and voluntary sector, culminating in *the Public Services (Social Value) Act 2012 (Department of Communities and Local Government* 2012*)*. Here, we see links to the burgeoning literature around public service dominant logics (Alford 2016; Osborne et al. 2016; Radnor et al. 2016) and emerging New Public Governance (Osborne 2006, 2010; Skelcher 2004).

Local government has also been subject to legislation and guidance around electoral and democratic reforms (Department of Communities and Local Government 2011c; DTLR 2000); engagement with communities (Department of Communities and Local Government 2006, 2008), and creating more open public services (Cabinet Office 2011, 2014). As we have previously mentioned, these reforms need to be seen in the context of changes to the way English local government is assessed and reviewed. These included the abolition of the Audit Commission (Pickles 2013), the revised audit arrangements (Department of Communities and Local Government 2014) and the view that 'armchair auditors' would emerge to fill the gap (DCLG 2011c). As we go to press, we are still waiting for this army of accountability-motivated residents to contribute significantly to the holes left by the removal of professional audit.

As we have argued above, transparency and accountability are not completely synonymous, and the coalition government's additional transparency fails to substitute adequately for accountability when it comes to the management of local government services. In part, we argue, this stems from a lack of capacity and capability in the 'amateur' end of the auditing world, and both the preponderance of financial auditing and the deregulation of much of the performance assessment regime in local government. The impact of austerity on budgets (Local Government Association 2015), and hence service levels, is now also a dominant force; sustainability in public services has become a key battleground for accountability. The inability to specify future outcomes (i.e. prospective accountability) and the removal of much of the financial ring-fencing of local government budgets has challenged the way we perceive these essential public services and whether they deliver 'value for money'—itself a concept that would benefit from further consideration (McKevitt 2015); a cynical perspective might ponder whether this coincidental or ideologically-driven.

Thus, we find ourselves facing a local government sector with fewer resources for delivery (both financial and human), increasing levels of demand for costly, individualised services around social care, and a minimal set of regulatory processes to understand how well those 650+ services are delivering. Recent examples have outlined some of the challenges facing local public services, and local government in particular, e.g. Northamptonshire County Council's declaration that the council will not be able to deliver a balanced budget (Northamptonshire County Council 2018). The risks of these challenges are perhaps inadequately understood at present and our findings suggest that this situation is likely to get worse.

Whilst early criticisms of the regulatory mechanisms of CPA and CAA are easily found (Broadbent 2003; McLean et al. 2007; Wilson 2004) and the use of performance management was clearly subject to some 'gaming' (Bevan and Hood 2006; Radnor 2011), it is also clear that overall accountability to the public has been diminished by their removal. We would also contend that the removal of contractual-style forms of accountability, such as public service agreements and local public service agreements where central and local government agree on the achievement of specific targets in return for additional funding, similarly limit the scope of accountability.

Local government, therefore, presents us with somewhat of an oxymoron in relation to accountability. An enormously diverse range of accountability mechanisms can be deployed, whilst the sector aligns closely with the concept of accountability as a *virtue* (Bovens et al. 2014). Whilst New Labour reforms attempted to lock in performance outcomes to funding and regulatory assessments, post-2010 this has been significantly reduced. Whilst this reduction has been welcomed by some (Glennon 2017; Leach 2010; McLean et al. 2007), the longer-term impact of the scale of diluting performance accountability is yet to be understood, although it has clearly raised concerns at the NAO (2014a).

However, we contend that a more granular approach to embedding a variety of accountability mechanisms may yet help local authorities to hold conversations with communities, and to have a more constructive dialogue between political and managerial leadership within authorities. The success of this may well depend on how much effort can be placed into developing more prospective accountability mechanisms, and new approaches to service design that embrace citizen and service user relationships with managerial and political institutions.

CONCLUSION

For English local government, this chapter has discussed five themes with regards to accountability and transparency arrangements. The themes speak to an important global debate beyond local government in both the research and practice of public management about public assurance, value for money and underlying performance management arrangements (Moynihan 2008; Hood 2010; Bovens et al. 2014; Ferry and Eckersley 2015a; Van Dooren et al. 2015).

It is implicitly acknowledged in this chapter that professionalised accountability—through professionally qualified auditors—costs money and time. In advanced western liberal democracies, the perception is that transparency is relatively less expensive through the capacity and capability of the internet to disseminate large quantities of data that citizens readily have access to for potential analytical exercises. It is, therefore, an attractive option in times of austerity and financial cutbacks for policymakers and practitioners to reduce professionalised accountability in terms of professionally qualified auditors as a means to save money and promote transparency as a surrogate.

However, an important point for policymakers, regulators and practitioners is that transparency is not a straightforward panacea for a reduction in professionalised accountability arrangements. Financial cutbacks alone should not be an acceptable reason to undermine and significantly reduce public accountability. This is because, in practice for many jurisdictions in advanced relatively wealthy western liberal democracies, any significant loss of professional capacity and capability regarding information and its interrogation is unlikely to be made up for by an army of armchair auditors that critically analyse and interpret raw data—citizens may perceive that they have better things to do, even assuming they had the ability to do it. Additionally, any savings in the cost of professionalised audits reduction may be more than eaten up by reduced value for money.

It is easy to appreciate (if not agree with) how financial conformance has been allowed to become the main focus of a reduced professionalised accountability apparatus as part of cutback management under austerity, especially given the requirement on local authorities to have a balanced budget for revenue and expenditure. The problem is that such arrangements are not adequate for the assessment of value for money or for assessing the financial resilience or sustainability of public services. This is because such arrangements provide significant challenges for governance, leadership and strategic alignment in managing risk. Indeed systemic 'service' failure becomes a concern when the budget becomes the sole focus. This problem is only exacerbated as reporting is partial, scrutiny variable and quality assurance reducing. The focus becomes the current financial position—and the ability to absorb and adapt financially—rather than a comprehensive view of performance.

Early intervention mechanisms are essential if public services fail or significantly underperform. In England, the local government sector has been proactive in devising its own SLI initiative. Nevertheless, this requires careful monitoring and considerable improvement if it is to be robust and ultimately even its proponents accept the central state may still be required to intervene in individual cases (Bennett et al. 2014).

Inevitably, any changes in accountability and transparency arrangements change the risk profile with regards to value for money. Operationally it is more difficult to adapt to unforeseen circumstances if funding arrangements have limited flexibility. The sustainable management of financial and other resources also becomes more difficult to ascertain when reporting focuses primarily on financial elements, when performance management arrangements are relatively weaker than what went before, and when information is insufficient and inadequate to make judgements about the robustness of value for money.

The discussion around the adequacy of accountability, transparency, and public assurance arrangements must, therefore, be embraced by practitioners and policymakers alike. If we are to have value for money public services, which the citizen has the right to expect, then arrangements to properly assess operational performance are just as important and must complement those for financial conformance. This should be the case whether public money is being used during austerity or in a period of growth. Essentially, our view contends that in a liberal democracy, the assurance of the public that government is providing appropriate stewardship of public money is sacrosanct, but so should be value for money.

REFERENCES

Ahrens, T., & Ferry, L. (2018). Institutional Entrepreneurship, Practice Memory, and Cultural Memory: Choice and Creativity in the Pursuit of Endogenous Change of Local Authority Budgeting. *Management Accounting Research, 38*, 12–21.

Ahrens, T., Ferry, L., & Khalifa, R. (2018). The Hybridising of Financial and Service Expertise in English Local Authority Budget Control: A Practice Perspective. *Qualitative Research in Accounting and Management* (Forthcoming).

Alford, J., & O'Flynn, J. (Eds.). (2012). *Rethinking Public Service Delivery: Managing with External Providers*. Basingstoke: Palgrave Macmillan.

Alford, J. (2016). Co-Production, Interdependence and Publicness: Extending Public Service-Dominant Logic. *Public Management Review, 18*, 673–691.

Ashworth, R., Boyne, G., & Delbridge, R. (2007). Escape from the Iron Cage? Organizational Change and Isomorphic Pressures in the Public Sector. *Journal of Public Administration Research and Theory, 19*(1), 165–187.

Audit Commission. (2002). *The Comprehensive Performance Assessment Framework for Single Tier and County Councils*. London: Audit Commission.

Audit Commission. (2005). *Comprehensive Performance Assessment: The Harder Test*. London: Audit Commission.

Audit Commission. (2009). *Comprehensive Area Assessment: The Framework*. London: Audit Commission.

Ball, A., & Seal, W. (2005). Social Justice in a Cold Climate: Could Social Accounting Make a Difference? In *Accounting Forum* (Vol. 4, pp. 455–473). Elsevier.

Behn, R. D. (2001). *Rethinking Democratic Accountability*. Washington, DC: Brookings Institution Press.

Bennett, M., Allen, T., Grace, C., & Martin, S. (2014). *Self, Sector or Centre? Approaches to Turnaround*. London: LGA.

Bevan, G., & Hood, C. (2006). What's Measured Is What Matters: Targets and Gaming in the English Public Health Care System. *Public Administration, 84*(3), 517–538.

Bovens, M., Goodin, R. E., & Schillemans, T. (2014). *The Oxford Handbook of Public Accountability*. Oxford: Oxford University Press.

Broadbent, J. (2003). Comprehensive Performance Assessment: The Crock of Gold at the End of the Performance Rainbow? *Public Money and Management, 23*, 5–8.

Cabinet Office. (2011). *Open Public Services (White Paper)*. London: TSO.

Cabinet Office. (2014). Open Public Services 2014. London: TSO.

Centre for Public Scrutiny. (2014). What Rotherham and Mid-Staffordshire Tell Us About Public Scrutiny and Where It Is Lacking. Centre for Public

Scrutiny. Retrieved March 27, 2018, from http://www.cfps.org.uk/ publications?item=11669&offset=0.

Centre for Public Scrutiny. (2015). *Annual Review 2014–2015*. Centre for Public Scrutiny. Retrieved March 26, 2018, from http://www.cfps.org.uk/ publications?item=11649&offset=0.

Centre for Public Scrutiny. (2018). *Local Public Accounts Committee Discussion Paper. Why Is It needed? What Will It Deliver?* Centre for Public Scrutiny. Retrieved March 26, 2018, from https://www.cfps.org.uk/wp-content/ uploads/CfPS-Local-Public-Accounts-Committees-v3.pdf.

Christensen, T., & Laegreid, P. (Eds.). (2011). *The Ashgate Research Companion to New Public Management*. Farnham: Ashgate.

DCLG (2006). Strong and Prosperous Communities (White Paper). London: TSO.

DCLG. (2007). *Local Government and Public Involvement in Health Act (2007)*. London: TSO.

DCLG. (2008). *Communities in Control: Real People, Real Power*. London: TSO.

DCLG. (2010). *Pickles Outlines Plans to Abolish Regional Government*. London: Department for Communities and Local Government.

DCLG. (2011a). *Armchair Auditors Are Here to Stay*. London: TSO.

DCLG. (2011b). *Best Value Statutory Guidance*. London: TSO.

DCLG (2011c). *Localism Act (2011)*. London: TSO.

DCLG. (2012). *Public Services (Social Value) Act (2012)*, C3. London: TSO.

DCLG. (2014). *Local Audit and Accountability Act (2014)*. London: TSO.

DCLG. (2015a). *Revised Best Value Statutory Guidance*. London: TSO.

DCLG. (2015b). *Local Government Transparency Code*. London: TSO.

DETR. (1999). *Best Value and Audit Commission Performance Indicators for 2000/2001: Volume One: The Performance Indicators*. London: TSO.

DTLR. (2000). *Local Government Act (2000)*. London: TSO.

DTLR. (2001). *Strong Local Leadership-Quality Public Services*. London: TSO.

Ellwood, S. (2014). Debate: Autonomy, Governance, Accountability and a New Audit Regime. *Public Money & Management, 34*(2), 139–141.

Etzioni, A. (2014). The Limits of Transparency. *Public Administration Review, 74*(6), 687–688.

Ferry, L., Coombs, H., & Eckersley, P. (2017). Budgetary Stewardship, Innovation and Working Culture: Identifying the Missing inGredient in English and Welsh Local Authorities' Recipes for Austerity Management. *Financial Accountability & Management, 33*(2), 220–243.

Ferry, L., & Eckersley, P. M. (2011). Budgeting and Governing for Deficit Reduction in the UK Public Sector: Act One 'the Comprehensive Spending Review'. *Journal of Finance and Management in Public Services, 10*(1), 14–23.

Ferry, L., & Eckersley, P. (2012). Budgeting and Governing for Deficit Reduction in the UK Public Sector: Act 2 'the Annual Budget'. *Public Money & Management, 32*(2), 119–126.

Ferry, L., & Eckersley, P. (2015a). Accountability and Transparency: A Nuanced Response to Etzioni. *Public Administration Review, 75*(1), 11–12.

Ferry, L., & Eckersley, P. (2015b). Budgeting and Governing for Deficit Reduction in the UK Public Sector: Act Three 'Accountability and Audit Arrangements'. *Public Money Manage, 35*(3), 203–210.

Ferry, L., Eckersley, P., & Van Dooren, W. (2015a). Local Taxation and Spending as a Share of GDP in Large Western European Countries. *Environment and Planning A, 47*(9), 1779–1780.

Ferry, L., Eckersley, P., & Zakaria, Z. (2015b). Accountability and Transparency in English Local Government: Moving From 'Matching Parts' to 'Awkward Couple'? *Financial Accountability & Management, 31*(3), 345–361.

Glennon, R. (2017). *The 'Death of Improvement': An Exploration of the Legacy of Performance and Service Improvement Reform in English Local Authorities, 1997–2017.* PhD, Loughborough University.

Glennon, R., Hodgkinson, I. R., Knowles, J., Radnor, Z., & Bateman, N. (2018). The Aftermath of Modernisation: Examining the Impact of a Change Agenda on Local Government Employees in the UK. *Australian Journal of Public Administration* (Forthcoming).

Goldfinch, S., & Wallis, J. O. E. (2010). Two Myths of Convergence in Public Management Reform. *Public Administration, 88*(4), 1099–1115.

Grant Thornton. (2015). *Local Government Governance Review. All Aboard?* Slough: Grant Thornton.

Gray, A., Jenkins, B. (1993). Codes of Accountability in the New Public Sector. *Accounting, Auditing & Accountability Journal, 6*(3) 52–67.

Hood, C. (2010). Accountability and Transparency: Siamese Twins, Matching Parts, Awkward Couple? *West European Politics, 33*, 989–1009.

Hodgkinson, I. R., Hughes, P., Hughes, M., & Glennon, R. (2017). Does Ownership Matter for Service Delivery Value? An Examination of Citizens' Service Satisfaction. *Public Management Review, 19*(8), 1206–1220.

Hopwood, A. (1984). Accounting and the Pursuit of Efficiency. In A. Hopwood & C. Tomkins (Eds.), *Issues in Public Sector Accounting.* Oxford: Philip Allan.

House of Commons Communities and Local Government Committee. (2011). *Select Committee: Audit and Inspection of Local Authorities* (Fourth Report of Session 2010–2012). London.

House of Commons Public Accounts Committee. (2015). *Financial Sustainability of Local Authorities, Thirty-Fourth Report of Session 2014–2015.* Norwich: Public Accounts Committee.

Leach, S. (2010). The Audit Commission's View of Politics: A Critical Evaluation of the CPA Process. *Local Government Studies, 36*, 445–461.

Le Grand, J., Wood, A., & Gibb, M. (2013). *Report to the Secretary of State for Education on Ways Forward for Children's Services in Doncaster*. Retrieved August 12, 2015.

LGA. (2011). *Taking the Lead: Self-Regulation and Improvement in Local Government*. London: Local Government Association.

LGA. (2014). *Evaluation of Sector-Led Improvement*. London: Local Government Association.

LGA. (2015). *Taking Stock: Where Next with Sector-Led Improvement?* London: Local Government Association.

Lowndes, V., & Pratchett, L. (2012). Local Governance Under the Coalition Government: Austerity, Localism and the 'Big Society'. *Local Government Studies, 38*(1), 21–40.

Magd, H., & Curry, A., (2003). Benchmarking: Achieving Best Value in Public Sector Organisations. *Benchmarking: An International Journal, 10*(3), 261–286.

McKevitt, D. (2015). Debate: Value for Money—In Search of a Definition. *Public Money & Management, 35*(2), 99–100.

Mclean, I., Haubrich, D., & Gutiérrez-Romero, R. (2007). The Perils and Pitfalls of Performance Measurement: The CPA Regime for Local Authorities in England. *Public Money and Management, 27*, 111–118.

Micheli, P., & Neely, A. (2010). Performance Measurement in the Public Sector in England: Searching for the Golden Thread. *Public Administration Review, 70*(4), 591–600.

Molnár, M. (2008). The Accountability Paradigm: Standards of Excellence: Theory and Research Evidence from Hungary. *Public Management Review, 10*(1), 127–137.

Moynihan, D. P. (2008). *The Dynamics of Performance Management: Constructing Information and Reform*. Washington, DC: Georgetown University Press.

Mulgan, R. (2000). Comparing Accountability in the Public and Private Sectors. *Australian Journal of Public Administration, 59*(1), 87–97.

Murphy, P. (2014). 15 The Development of the Strategic State and the Performance Management of Local Authorities in England. *Strategic Management in Public Organizations: European Practices and Perspectives*, 243.

Murphy, P., & Jones, M. (2016). Building the Next Model for Intervention and Turnaround in Poorly Performing Local Authorities in England. *Local Government Studies, 42*(5), 698–716.

NAO. (2014a). *Financial Sustainability of Local Authorities*. London: National Audit Office.

NAO. (2014b). *The Impact of Funding Reductions on Local Authorities*. London: National Audit Office.

Osborne, S. P. (2006). The New Public Governance? *Public Management Review, 8*, 377–387.

Osborne, S. P. (2010). Delivering Public Services: Time for a new theory? *Public Management Review, 12*, 1–10.

Osborne, S. P., Radnor, Z., & Strokosch, K. (2016). Co-Production and the Co-Creation of Value in Public Services: A suitable case for treatment? *Public Management Review, 18*, 639–653.

Ospina, S., Cunill Grau, N., & Zaltsman, A. (2004). Performance Evaluation, Public Management Improvement and Democratic Accountability: Some Lessons from Latin America. *Public Management Review, 6*(2), 229–251.

Pickles, E. (2013). Local Government Association Conference Speech. *Local Government Association*, 3 July 2013.

Radnor, Z. (2011). Hitting the Target and Missing the Point? Developing an Understanding of Organizational Gaming. In W. Van Dooren & S. Van de Walle (Eds.), *Performance Information in the Public Sector: How It Is Used* (pp. 98–109). Basingstoke: Palgrave Macmillan.

Radnor, Z., Osborne, S., & Glennon, R. (2016). Public Management Theory. In C. Ansell & J. Torfing (Eds.), *Handbook on Theories of Governance*. Cheltenham: Edward Elgar.

Rashman, L., & Radnor, Z., (2005). Learning to Improve: Approaches to Improving Local Government Services. *Public Money and Management, 25*(1), 19–26.

Raudla, R., Savi, R., & Randma-Liiv, T. (2013). Literature Review on Cutback Management.

Rhodes, R. A. W. (1981). *Control and Power in Central-Local Government Relations*. Gower and Brookfield, VT: Ashgate.

Seal, W. (2003). Modernity, Modernization and the Deinstitutionalization of Incremental Budgeting in Local Government. *Financial Accountability & Management, 19*, 93–116.

Seal, W., & Ball, A. (2005). Regulating Corporate Performance and the Managerialization of Local Politics. *International Public Management Review, 6*(1), 117–138.

Seal, W., & Ball, A. (2011). Interpreting the Dynamics of Public Sector Budgeting: A Dialectic of Control Approach. *Financial Accountability & Management, 27*(4), 409–436.

Shaoul, J., Stafford, A., & Stapleton, P. (2012). Accountability and Corporate Governance of Public Private Partnerships. *Critical Perspectives on Accounting, 23*(3), 213–229.

Skelcher, C. (2004). The New Governance of Communities. In G. Stoker & D. Wilson (Eds.), *British Local Government into the 21st Century*. Basingstoke: Palgrave Macmillan.

Svara, J. H. (2001). The Myth of the Dichotomy: Complementarity of Politics and Administration in the Past and Future of Public Administration. *Public Administration Review, 61*(2), 176–183.

Timmins, N., & Gash, T. (2014). *Dying to Improve: The Demise of the Audit Commission and Other Improvement Agencies.* London: Institute for Government.

Treasury, H. M. (2010). *Budget 2010.* London: HM Treasury.

Van Dooren, W., Bouckaert, G., & Halligan, J. (2015). *Performance Management in the Public Sector.* London: Routledge.

Warren, M. E. (2014). Accountability and Democracy. In M. Bovens, R. E. Goodin, & T. Schillemans (Eds.), *The Oxford Handbook of Public Accountability* (pp. 39–54). Oxford: Oxford University Press.

Wildavsky, A. (1975). *Budgeting: A Comparative Theory of Budgetary Processes.* Boston: Little, Brown.

Willems, T., & Van Dooren, W. (2012). Coming to Terms with Accountability: Combining Multiple Forums and Functions. *Public Management Review, 14*(7), 1011–1036.

Wilson, J. (2004). Comprehensive Performance Assessment-Springboard or Dead-Weight? *Public Money and Management, 24,* 63–68.

Wilson, D., & Game, C. (2011). *Local Government in the United Kingdom* (5th ed.). London: Palgrave Macmillan.

CHAPTER 4

Health and Social Care

Laurence Ferry, Peter Murphy and Russ Glennon

Abstract This is the second of the four chapters applying the two models to particular sectors. In England, Health and Social Care are two interrelated public services with both the largest budgets and projected rises in future service demand, mostly because of long-term factors outside of their short-term control, such as demographic changes. The *Health and Social Care Act 2012* represented the most significant systematic change to the operational environment and institutional architecture of healthcare since the introduction of the welfare state. Since implementation, there have been continual attempts to mitigate its baleful impact on accountability, service delivery, and public assurance. Although the *'matching parts'* of accountability and transparency should have become clearer in healthcare, we find that it has actually become more opaque.

Keywords Health and social care · Healthcare management Accountability · Public assurance

INTRODUCTION

The development of accountability and performance management in health and social care followed closely that of local government under the previous New Labour reforms. Unlike local government, however, spending on the Department of Health, and particularly on the NHS, was one of the so-called 'protected' areas of public expenditure under

© The Author(s) 2019
P. Murphy et al., *Public Service Accountability*,
https://Doi.org/10.1007/978-3-319-93384-9_4

the coalition government. Nevertheless, the financial challenges facing both the NHS and social care continued to increase and are widely anticipated to get worse in the foreseeable future. In addition, 'real' investment in health and social care did in fact decrease, albeit at a much slower rate than in local government.

The *Health and Social Care Act 2012* represented the most significant systematic change to the operational environment and institutional architecture of the NHS since the service was established over 70 years ago. This took place in addition to financial challenge that was unprecedented in the history of an NHS that had experienced only increased investment since its inception. This chapter will use the framework outlined in Chapter 2 to evaluate the implications of structural as well as financial reforms for the NHS and health and social care.

The importance of NHS accountability and transparency arrangements being 'fit for purpose' recently came in for 'specific' attention given resource pressures (Ham et al. 2015), structural fragmentation (NAO 2014, 2015a, b, 2016) and the changing audit landscape (Ellwood and Garcia-Lacalle 2015). This chapter, therefore, investigates the relationship between accountability and transparency, and how they have been undermined by reporting changes and structural fragmentation.

As outlined in Chapter 1, accountability as a concept appears easily understood, although it resists narrow definitions. Added to this, numerous related concepts such as transparency and governance have overlapping meanings.

The Coalition's NHS Inheritance

The NHS was founded in 1948 to provide national healthcare for the UK population. Prior to the economic crises of the 1970s, it was a heavily centralised bureaucracy with hierarchical, financial, and performance arrangements (Gebreiter 2016) and a strong sense of political control. Nye Bevan, the Labour minister considered the father of the NHS, famously said, '*If a bedpan is dropped on a hospital floor in Tredegar, its noise should resound in the Palace of Westminster*' (Bevan 1948, cited in Nairne 1984). Ministerial accountability was thus placed at the heart of the NHS as an institution.

Over the following decades, as the population, scope of medical care, and demand grew, the financial sustainability of healthcare became a recurrent and significant political issue facing successive governments; many of these implemented service changes with accountability implications (Gebreiter and Ferry 2016; Ferry and Scarparo 2015). This centralised and hierarchical framework began to fragment in the 1980s and 1990s as a consequence of the New Public Management (NPM) reforms of Thatcher's and Major's Conservative governments. These enthusiastically embraced approaches including internal market-like structures, increased private provision and private finance initiatives (PFI) that sought to move government borrowing off the public debt books (Propper et al. 2008) and further engage the private sector in the delivery of public services (Broadbent et al. 2003). These served to 'muddy the waters' of accountability by adding in additional layers of principal/agent accountability.

In 1997, New Labour swept to power with a huge majority and a mandate to implement significant change. Modernisation of public services was a key part of their reform agenda (Glennon et al. 2018). Contrary to expectations, and somewhat counter-intuitively, New Labour continued along this trajectory of greater private sector involvement in public sector delivery. This was implemented via both privatisation through PFI and PPP arrangements and introducing an era of managerialism by a targets-driven policy and performance management system that made accountability a process of targets, box-ticking, and audit trails (Ferry and Scarparo 2015; Bevan and Hood 2006).

The culture of targets was a fundamental part of New Labour public sector reform, in which a seemingly ever-increasing range of targets to drive the delivery of the NHS was matched by public communication and sharing of data, thus generating a '*matching parts*' arrangement. Ostensibly, this was so the government could reassure citizens that increased taxation from investment was being put to good use (Ferry and Scarparo 2015). At the same time, and in direct contrast, these arrangements were undermined by fragmented organisational structures (Bevan and Hood 2006; Chang 2009, 2015).

New Labour's approach was characterised by an increasingly centralised bureaucracy through both hierarchical accountability and transparency. This provided *matching parts*, but direct hierarchical accountability was made more difficult by conflicting interventions. For example, the performance management framework and audit data were made publicly available. This contrasts with the opacity of collaborative agreements and commissioning from the private sector (including PFI and PPPs) that had been a continuation of the earlier Conservative government's policies. This fragmentation also made accountability for public money and operations more complex and opaque (Shaoul et al. 2011). There were also financial issues for accountability and transparency. Indeed, New Labour had employed PFI in delivering the biggest hospital building programme in NHS history. PFIs were also criticised for storing up debts to be met by future governments. In addition, New Labour was accused of awarding 'lucrative' salary and wage increases alongside workload reductions that masqueraded as productivity gains under the 'agenda for change' initiative. Furthermore, New Labour had acquired a reputation for blaming overspends on hospital mismanagement and suggesting there was more than enough money in the NHS. Despite increased spending during this period, serious concerns arose over patient care and safety, most notably after the Mid Staffordshire scandal (Francis 2013).

The fragmentation of structural accountability mechanisms, cost implications from PFI and staff remuneration, issues over safety and quality, and concerns of blame and spin would re-emerge in a 'blame game' around the financial sustainability, accountability and transparency of the NHS under the coalition government from 2010 to 2015.

Coalition Government 2010–2015

In 2010, the Conservative-led coalition inherited New Labour's increasingly re-centralised and hierarchical bureaucracy that employed a *matching parts* arrangement of accountability and transparency but which was accompanied by other arrangements that made lines of 'direct' accountability even more complex.

The coalition's response to this was the *Health and Social Care Bill*, developed whilst in opposition, and subsequently steered through parliament, where objections surrounded fears of greater marketisation, privatisation, and ultimately 'the end of the NHS'. Of particular controversy was the goal to limit the Health Secretary's accountability for the NHS, which met with strong opposition both inside and outside parliament. To address some of these criticisms, and to take account of concerns of the coalition's partners, the Liberal Democrats, the Bill was amended in the House of Lords following detailed discussions brokered by Earl Howe. The final Act would be a political compromise. Nevertheless, the *Health and Social Care Act 2012* fundamentally changed structural relationships within the NHS and, in particular, the establishment of NHS England as a non-departmental public body; this severed the hierarchical direct accountability link that could be traced back to Bevan.

In the same parliament, the *Local Audit and Accountability Act 2014* crystalised the abolition of the Audit Commission and passed financial audit responsibilities to the National Audit Office (NAO). Nevertheless, the revised system retained performance management arrangements and quality checks, as well as continuity in the transparency of hospital performance information; the *matching parts* remained largely in place.

However, the direct, hierarchical arrangements that had already begun to fragment under New Labour were then significantly ruptured by the coalition's establishment of NHS England. For example, despite manifesto assurances to the contrary (Conservative Party 2010), and longest formal consultation process ever conducted by a UK government, the coalition's *Health and Social Care Act 2012* resulted in comprehensive restructuring of the NHS (Timmins 2012) and generated damning criticism, especially from the King's Fund (Ham et al. 2015).

Under the act, the Department of Health (DoH) remained responsible for the overall policy, design, and stewardship of the service. But the act transferred 'direct' responsibility for 'managing' the health service from the DoH to the new NHS England (formerly the NHS Commissioning Board), along with responsibility for the majority of funding. NHS England now passes much of this on to local clinical commissioning groups (CCGs) for locally commissioned services, with some responsibility retained for nationally commissioned services.

CCGs bought in secondary care, community services, mental health, and rehabilitation services for their local populations. Other healthcare services were also directly commissioned by NHS England, namely primary care, including general practitioner (GP) services and specialist services such as dentistry, community pharmacy, etc.

As well as contradicting the mantra of 'no top-down reorganisation of the NHS' (Lansley 2007), this reform also generated a significant lack of clarity about the accountability relationship between the DoH and NHS England, a concern shared by health campaigning organisation, the King's Fund, attributed in part to policy compromises generated by the coalition process (Ham et al. 2015).

In contrast, fears that ministers would no longer be held accountable for the NHS under the new arrangements were ill-founded. Lansley's reforms proved too controversial and he was replaced in September 2012 by Jeremy Hunt. Hunt took a close interest in NHS performance, and established an approach of damage limitation, ignoring many reforms and particularly those concerning competition and choice as drivers of NHS performance improvement. In the wake of the Francis report into the Mid Staffordshire NHS Foundation Trust's care failures (Francis 2013), he became a champion of patient interests.

At the local level, the NHS outcomes framework also sits alongside the outcomes frameworks for adult social care and public health, both of which relate to local government as well as the NHS. This requires close working together and came at a time when local government was experiencing severe financial cutbacks from the coalition government's austerity policy, putting intense pressure on budgets and staffing (Ferry et al. 2015).

Local health institutions struggled to assimilate the accountability, governance, and performance arrangements. For example, structural arrangements for the health service had further complexities, as CCGs alongside local authorities and local HealthWatch made up new health and wellbeing boards as part of collaboration arrangements for the new integrated public health service, known as Public Health England. They collaborated with each other and had responsibility for joint strategic needs assessments and the development of joint health and wellbeing strategies (Murphy 2013). Although DoH was responsible for securing funds for adult social care through the spending review, it was the DCLG that became accountable for allocation of those funds to local authorities, adding further complexity into the funding of the structures. Indeed, in October 2013 the Kings Fund reported,

> There is little sign as yet that health and wellbeing boards have begun to grapple with the immediate and urgent strategic challenges facing their local health and social care systems. (The King's Fund 2013)

NHS audit arrangements under the Local Audit and Accountability Act 2014 became more localised and fragmented, echoing the move away from 'direct' accountability as seen in the delegation of health services management to NHS England. For example, the coalition government announced the abolition of the Audit Commission and its local counterpart, district audit (e.g. local) (Ellwood and Garcia-Lacalle 2012), thus repealing the Audit Commission Act 1998. This introduced changes to external auditing and financial reporting arrangements that affected local delivered public services including local NHS delivery Trusts. It transferred responsibility to the NAO for auditing accounts of DoH and its arm's-length bodies, including NHS England. Yet the centralised audit system for CCGs is through a local audit by an accredited provider and in the case of foundation trusts, each trust can appoint an auditor from a body of accountants approved by the Secretary of State; audit arrangements are now as fragmented as the delivery arrangements.

Conversely, the performance management regime remained centralised, although subject to considerable changes altering 'direct' accountability arrangements regarding planning and performance. In particular, the coalition government abandoned the system of public service agreement (PSA) targets within central government, closed government regional offices and discontinued local area agreements (LAAs). This substantially changed the legacy system of mutually agreed local and central objectives and targets for public services at the community level, problematising the trajectory towards enhanced co-production.

External inspectorates also witnessed changes that reflected (in practice, at least) the weakening of hierarchical 'direct' accountability seen elsewhere. Monitor acted as the regulator for providers of health services and the Care Quality Commission (CQC) was the independent regulator of all health and social care in England, replacing the Healthcare Commission and Commission for Social Care Inspection (CSCI), respectively, in 2009.

CQC focused on annual 'quality accounts' contained within CQC Annual Health Checks, and Monitor focused on planning, overview, and reporting requirements. Initially introduced in 2009, quality accounts originally allowed considerable discretion as to their content, and reports were published by service providers on their own websites rather than centrally. This meant they were arguably more susceptible to gaming by organisations in order to give a flattering picture of performance. Additionally, reports could be buried on organisational websites, thus reducing transparency, and undermining benchmarking and retrospective accountability.

Over time, however, the contents of quality accounts have become more proscribed and standardised. In 2013, the CQC announced a broad aim for a new CQC inspection regime for hospital inspection. This involved returning to a system of more specialist inspections, with greater involvement of staff and the public. Monitor's role was also clarified as being to support patient interests by promoting the provision of healthcare services that are economical, efficient, and effective, and to maintain or improve their quality. It does this primarily through its risk assessment frameworks (RAFs) and responsibility for payments and financial systems operating within the NHS and its suppliers. This arguably marks a return to the previous ethos of external inspection regimes, a pattern that may be in the process of being replicated elsewhere, e.g. fire and rescue (see Chapter 6).

There were changes, too, in the focus on transparency. The coalition continued the duty of Freedom of Information Act requirements for the NHS. A requirement was placed on all NHS organisations to publish details online of all expenditure over £25,000, contrasting with the local government requirement to spell out items over £500. Reforms also saw other data publishing requirements including more clinician-level data, overarching clinical indicators, extending the friends and family test, and linking clinical data from GPs.

However, these arrangements were and are being tested. Scandals relating to patient care in Mid Staffordshire Hospitals Trust (Francis 2013), as well as examples from a decade before (Kennedy 2001) have proved challenging, both politically and institutionally. Added to this, a growing number of hospitals have been reported by Monitor to be in financial difficulties, often as a result of (now) historical PFI contracts, as well as increasing demand levels, challenging efficiency targets and knock on impacts from cuts in local authority social care budgets leading to so-called bed blocking by elderly patients in particular. Figure 4.1 identifies the change in ability to demonstrate accountability during the period 2010–2015.

This places the sector in a challenging position regarding external, retrospective accountability, particularly at the systemic level. A report by the House of Commons' Public Administration Select Committee (2014) was particularly scathing. It raised concerns about the coherence, transparency, and navigability of the healthcare system for patients and the public, and suggested overall levels of performance, quality, safety, and financial resilience were unclear and unacceptable. The report blamed relationships between the DoH and NHS England in part, saying they were 'extremely complicated and still evolving'. In response, Jeremy Hunt beefed up the CQC's role, emphasising the need for greater transparency and accountability for performance. Working with

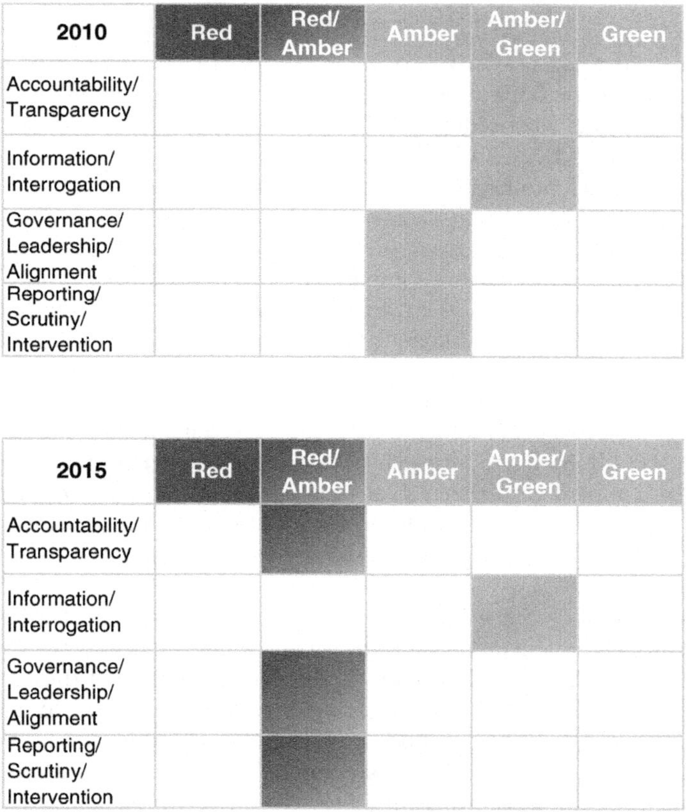

2010	Red	Red/Amber	Amber	Amber/Green	Green
Accountability/Transparency				▨	
Information/Interrogation				▨	
Governance/Leadership/Alignment			▨		
Reporting/Scrutiny/Intervention				▨	

2015	Red	Red/Amber	Amber	Amber/Green	Green
Accountability/Transparency		▨			
Information/Interrogation				▨	
Governance/Leadership/Alignment		▨			
Reporting/Scrutiny/Intervention		▨			

Fig. 4.1 Health and Social Care: Public Assurance 2010–2015

Sir Simon Stevens (Chief Executive of NHS England), who took up post in April 2014, they focused more on NHS finances ahead of the 2015 general election to address the fact that more and more providers were incurring deficits and missing targets. In 2018, NHS funding and performance remain a political and public hot topic, further complicated by highly contested Brexit promises of additional funding.

EVALUATION OF ACCOUNTABILITY

The story of NHS reforms as outlined above is characterised by a move away from (or perhaps more accurately, a fragmentation of) a centrally controlled direct hierarchical mode and towards a more individualised, retrospective model. This is more closely aligned with mode one (service management) accountability as we term it in our evaluative model. The NHS and social care retain a degree of external regulation at the institutional level, via the two inspectorate bodies, but overall, we characterise them as lightly regulated in comparison with other forms of public service. The 1997–2010 focus on institutional comparisons (mode two in our model) has clearly weakened. Whilst there have been some attempts to develop actions that support mode three (facilitating continuous improvement), these have not been significant (Bevan 2006; Burgess and Radnor 2013; Radnor et al. 2012). This remains an area of weakness for the NHS. The contingent nature of service institutions and their demands, coupled with the centralisation of power in one part of the system (CCGs), and the dismantling of regulatory and improvement infrastructure capacity, have problematised the implementation of continuous improvement.

From a policy perspective, both accountability and transparency arrangements remained central to governance and management under all administrations between 2000 and 2015, but the effects of these need to be better understood when considering structural changes. In addition, health bodies still bear a democratic deficit at the local level, i.e. there are few opportunities for political engagement in policy and strategy development, although this situation is clearly different for social care and public health, which transferred back into local authority control.

The deregulation of the local area performance and accountability mechanisms that were overseen by the Audit Commission may also have left gaps in local accountability. The structural changes that created CCGs concentrated the power and control over future expenditure into smaller, more local, bodies, but arguably at the expense of systemic health development, i.e. a more pluralist health agenda. Similarly, the removal of contractual forms such as LAAs and PSAs have weakened the capacity for creating accountability frameworks within local public service delivery.

This can be seen as part of the move towards individualised, retrospective forms, and the NHS 'Friends and Family Test' is a clear example of this. The mandating of this 'performance' measure pushes accountability away from the governance body to create the right conditions for accountability and effective delivery and instead places this responsibility on the individual to complain about service failure.

Yet the narratives surrounding some of these changes do at least address some of the weaknesses facing the sector. The emphasis on co-production and quality standards address our fourth mode of accountability—generating the conditions for future accountability, if perhaps still operating at the individualistic level.

Politically, the government has had to recognise the level of resistance to NHS changes, as well as the problems generated by rising demand, ageing populations, and conflict points between different parts of the pathway of health and social care. These are policy, service, and financial problems that will have to be addressed; this has been exacerbated by high-profile scandals surrounding service failure.

It is important that clear lines of accountability are considered and established before policies are enacted and implemented, otherwise public services and public money are unlikely to remain subject to appropriate accountability, making financial, and performance sustainability more challenging to understand, let alone implement. Overall reductions in accountability have, as with local government, been addressed in theory by improvements in transparency. The ambition here appears to have been to move towards transparency supporting accountability. And yet the results suggest that these changes have not generated the improvements desired.

The complex structures, poorly integrated delivery mechanisms and opaque channels of responsibility have meant accountability and transparency arrangements have become less clear (NAO 2014; Ham et al. 2015). It has to be recognised in practice that performance indicators and targets can have benefits, but can also mask challenges of financial sustainability, unsustainable service levels, and poorly negotiated restructuring. Doing so only makes accountability relationships more complex and opaque.

It is clear that structural changes generated by the *Health and Social Care Act 2012* and the requirements of the Local Audit and Accountability Act 2014 have not facilitated either improved accountability or transparency. Future research must consider how accountability and transparency can be extended beyond the traditional hierarchical accountability structures of an NHS based on a public service delivery model so that new hybridised and distributed forms of delivery involving various forms of privatisation can be properly held to account.

CONCLUSIONS

This chapter explored how changes to structure and reporting could have implications for accountability and transparency arrangements. To do so it critically analysed arrangements in the NHS of England under the Conservative-led coalition government from 2010 to 2015.

New Labour embraced a reform agenda for the NHS and developed a symbiotic relationship between accountability and transparency, with transparency emphasised as a particular virtue (Bovens et al. 2014), and a sense of continuity with this approach emerged under the Conservative-led coalition government. The NHS did encounter changes to audit oversight following the abolition of the Audit Commission (Ellwood and Garcia-Lacalle 2012), but the fundamentals of accountability remained in place relative to other parts of the public services in England, i.e. it retained audit of both financial and performance areas and financial transparency with transactions published online for public scrutiny. The combination of mutually supportive accountability and transparency therefore appeared to continue. This was despite changes from the Local Audit and Accountability Act 2014 and recent changes in the inspectorates, as well as their role and focus of inspection. However, this has served to generate a dissonance of accountability. Mutually supportive accountability and transparency was most suited to a hierarchical accountability-based NHS. This linkage has been ruptured by more privatisation and the Conservative-led coalition government's establishment of NHS England by the *Health and Social Care Act 2012*. This disrupted the structures in place for hierarchically based accountability arrangements (House of Commons Public Administration Select Committee 2014; Ham et al. 2015).

The relationship between accountability and transparency in the NHS was perceived to be relatively strong compared to local government, where (non-democratic) forms of accountability were diluted and not adequately replaced by transparency. For example, Ferry et al. (2015) showed that local government arrangements for accountability (audit and performance management) were reduced and that to compensate, arrangements for financial transparency (transactions published online) were increased. This transparency, however, did not make up for the reductions in external accountability following the scrapping of the performance management system and the abolition of the Audit Commission; the anticipated army of citizens acting as 'armchair auditors' to make use of this increased transparency did not materialise.

The relationship between accountability and transparency in local government was, therefore, less mutually supportive. A cynical perspective might suggest different arrangements were desirable between local government and the NHS because funding was substantially reduced in local government, whilst health retained most of their budget and thus there were different expectations of the impact on performance. The coalition government did not want the impact on service performance to be made as clear.

However, the arrangements the NHS would have arguably been stronger had the centralised hierarchical bureaucracy-based system not been undermined by a legacy of fragmentation, delivered by Conservative, coalition, and New Labour administrations alike. The approval of the *Health and Social Care Act 2012* and *Local Audit and Accountability Act 2014* both contributed to this fragmentation, primarily through the passporting of operational responsibility to the new NHS England body, altering the direct line of accountability that had been present since the NHS's inception in 1948. By delegating operational responsibility, it can be argued that the government was trying to shift responsibility, and potential blame, onto NHS England. This may in some ways have mirrored the impact of austerity localism in local government, which was given more power over service determination, but not the funding capacity to meet expectations. We can perhaps see here a system of accountability and transparency in place for *'pinning down blame'*, rather than for genuine performance improvement.

However, the complexity and opaque structures have led to problems in assessing value for money and often determining responsibilities and ultimately *'pinning down blame'*. A NAO report highlighting the financial unsustainability of the NHS led to the House of Lords Select Committee in 2016 to consider the future of health services and a 2017 Public Accounts Committee to consider the financial sustainability of health services; both were largely critical.

The changes also mean that the healthcare system as a whole, and individual organisations and services within it—most notably the acute hospital trusts—are increasingly struggling to meet centrally set objectives and targets. In addition, inherited financial and service issues from

New Labour such as servicing PFI debt interest, favourable changes to staff terms and conditions, and the fallout from healthcare scandals such as Mid Staffs, made it easier for the coalition government to blame New Labour for the ills of the NHS.

In summary, therefore, the supportive relationship between transparency and accountability in the NHS should have made determining financial conformance and performance clearer, but instead has become more opaque. In particular, this was due to significant structural and operational changes from the *Health and Social Care Act 2012* and Local Audit and Accountability Act 2014 implemented at a time of financial restraint. For example, NHS England is at arm's-length from government, at least from a theoretical accountability perspective. The separation of direct accountability means responsibility is now not as clear as at the establishment of the NHS when Bevan rhetorically suggested a bedpan dropped in a hospital corridor anywhere in the country would have reverberations that echo in Whitehall.

REFERENCES

Bevan, G. (2006). Setting Targets for Health Care Performance: Lessons from a Case Study of the English NHS. *National Institute Economic Review, 197*(1), 67–79.

Bevan, G., & Hood, C. (2006). Health Policy: Have Targets Improved Performance in the English NHS? *BMJ, 332*(February), 419–422.

Bovens, M., Schillemans, T., & Goodin, R. E. (2014). Public Accountability. In M. Bovens, R. E. Goodin, & T. Schillemans (Eds.), *The Oxford Handbook of Public Accountability* (pp. 1–22). Oxford: Oxford University Press.

Broadbent, J., Gill, J., & Laughlin, R. (2003). Evaluating the Private Finance Initiative in the National Health Service in the UK. *Accounting, Auditing & Accountability Journal, 16*(3), 422–445.

Burgess, N., & Radnor, Z. (2013). Evaluating Lean in Healthcare. *International Journal of Health Care Quality Assurance, 26*(3), 220–235.

Chang, Lc. (2009). The Impact of Political Interests Upon the Formulation of Performance Measurements: The NHS Star Rating System. *Financial Accountability & Management, 25*(2), 145–165.

Chang, Lc. (2015). Accountability, Rhetoric, and Political Interests: Twists and Turns of NHS Performance Measurements. *Financial Accountability & Management, 31*(1), 41–68.

Conservative Party. (2010). *Invitation to Join the Government of Britain: The Conservative Manifesto 2010*. London.

Ellwood, S., & Garcia-Lacalle, J. (2012). New Development: Local Public Audit—The Changing Landscape. *Public Money Manage, 32*(5), 389–392.

Ellwood, S., & Garcia-Lacalle, J. (2015). The Removal of a Specialist Oversight Body for Local Public Audit: Insights from the Health Service in England. *Financial Accountability & Management, 31*(2), 219–242.

Ferry, L., Eckersley, P., & Zakaria, Z. (2015). Accountability and Transparency in English Local Government: Moving from 'Matching Parts' to 'Awkward Couple'? *Financial Accountability & Management, 31*(3), 345–361.

Ferry, L., & Scarparo, S. (2015). An Era of Governance Through Performance Management–New Labour's National Health Service from 1997 to 2010. *Accounting History Review, 25*(3), 219–238.

Francis, R. (2013). *Report of the Mid Staffordshire NHS Foundation Trust Public Inquiry Executive Summary.* London: The Stationery Office.

Gebreiter, F. (2016). "Comparing the Incomparable": Hospital Costing and the Art of Medicine in Post-war Britain. *The British Accounting Review, 48*(2), 257–268.

Gebreiter, F., & Ferry, L. (2016). Accounting and the 'Insoluble' Problem of Health-Care Costs. *European Accounting Review, 25*(4), 719–733.

Glennon, R., Hodgkinson, I. R., Knowles, J., Radnor, Z., & Bateman, N. (2018). The Aftermath of Modernisation: Examining the Impact of a Change Agenda on Local Government Employees in the UK. *Australian Journal of Public Administration* (Forthcoming).

Ham, C., Baird, B., Gregory, S., Jabbal, J., & Alderwick, H. (2015). *The NHS Under the Coalition Government. Part One: NHS Reform.* London: The King's Fund.

House of Commons Public Administration Select Committee. (2014). *Who's Accountable? Relationships Between Government and Arm's-Length Bodies.* Retrieved December 1, 2015, from http://www.publications.parliament.uk/pa/cm201415/cmselect/cmpubadm/110/11007.htm.

Kennedy, I. (2001). *Bristol Royal Infirmary Inquiry; Learning from Bristol: The Report of the Public Inquiry into Children's Heart Surgery at the Bristol Royal Infirmary 1984–1995.* London: The Stationary Office.

Lansley, A. (2007). *Conservative Party Press Release on NHS (Since Deleted).* London: Conservative Party.

Murphy, P. (2013). Public Health and Health and Wellbeing Boards: Antecedents, Theory and Development. *Perspectives in Public Health, 133*(5), 248–253.

Nairne, P. (1984). Parliamentary Control and Accountability in Public Participation in Health. In R. Maxwell & N. Weaver (Eds.), *Public Participation in Health: Towards a Clearer View* (Vol. 14, pp. 33–51). London: The King's Fund.

NAO. (2014). *The Financial Sustainability of NHS Bodies*. London: National Audit Office.

NAO. (2015a). *Confirmed Impacts: Helping to Improve Accountability in the Health System*. London: National Audit Office.

NAO. (2015b). *Sustainability and Financial Performance of Acute Hospital Trusts*. London: National Audit Office.

NAO. (2016). *Managing the Supply of NHS Clinical Staff in England*. London: National Audit Office.

Propper, C., Sutton, M., Whitnall, C., & Windmeijer, F. (2008). Did 'targets and Terror' Reduce Waiting Times in England for Hospital Care? *The B.E. Journal of Economic Analysis & Policy, 8*(2), 1–27.

Radnor, Z., Holweg, M., & Waring, J. (2012). Lean in Healthcare: The Unfilled Promise? *Social Science and Medicine, 74*(3), 364–371.

Shaoul, J., Stafford, A., & Stapleton, P. (2011). NHS Capital Investment and PFI: From Central Responsibility to Local Affordability. *Financial Accountability & Management, 27*(1), 1–17.

The King's Fund. (2013). *Health and Wellbeing Boards: One Year On*. London.

Timmins, N. (2012). *Never Again? Or the Story of the 2012 Health and Social Care Act*. London: The King's Fund/Institute for Government.

CHAPTER 5

Police

Peter Murphy, Laurence Ferry and Russ Glennon

Abstract Theresa May consider her police reforms in the period that she was Home Secretary to be one of the outstanding successes of the post-recession public sector reforms. The introduction of Police and Crime Commissioners, reform of HMIC, and the diminution of the institutional power of the police were central to these reforms. These reforms changed the nature of accountability arrangements for the 43 territorial police forces in England and Wales. These forces are controlled locally and deal with the vast majority of crimes, such as robbery, arson, theft, and assault. The analysis suggests that, as in healthcare, the year 2012 was a key turning point. Prior to 2012 accountability, transparency, and public assurance were diminishing, after 2012, we find that it has tended to improve.

Keywords Police reform · Accountability · Governance
Police and crime commissioners

INTRODUCTION

The current Prime Minister Theresa May considers her reforms of the police in the period that she was Home Secretary (2010–2016) to be one of the outstanding successes of the post-recession public sector reforms. The introduction of police and crime commissioners (PCCs), the reform of Her Majesty's Inspectorate of Constabulary (HMIC), and

© The Author(s) 2019
P. Murphy et al., *Public Service Accountability*,
https://doi.org/10.1007/978-3-319-93384-9_5

the diminution of the institutional power of the police were central to these reforms. Contrary to their own and others' expectations, the police also experienced a long-term reduction (in real terms) in both their absolute and relative share of public expenditure which was unprecedented under a Conservative government or Conservative-led coalition.

These financial constraints on and structural reforms to the police were reflected in local and national policing and impacted upon public service accountability, public assurance and value for money. This chapter will utilise the original evaluative framework and its constituent concepts, in order to review the implications and consequences for local policing between 2010 and 2015, before revisiting both this period and more recent changes through the lens of the new evaluative model outlined in Chapter 2.

This chapter will focus on how recent national government reforms have changed the nature of accountability arrangements for the 43 territorial police forces in England and Wales. These are the forces that controlled locally and deal with the vast majority of crimes, such as robbery, burglary, arson, theft, and assault. It does not relate to the special police forces, nor to Scotland or Northern Ireland, where similar, but different, arrangements are in place.

This chapter explores the conceptual nature of accountability, before analysing the evolution of various regimes that sought to monitor financial and operational performance and provide public assurance in relation to territorial police services. Although their original antecedents emerged during earlier Conservative administrations, these regimes developed rapidly under the New Labour administrations between 1997 and 2010, before being radically reformed by the Conservative-led coalition government that held office between May 2010 and May 2015.

The coalition reforms sought to improve accountability and transparency to citizens by introducing elected PCCs and giving the public greater access to data about the activities of their local force as part of the government's 'transparency' agenda. The government created the *www.police.uk* website for policing information and promised to create a similar site for fire and rescue services (FRSs) that would help the public 'to assess the performance of their local service … and … unleash armchair auditors to scrutinise and do their work on how their service is operating' (Lewis 2017).

Finally, they radically transformed the governance and operation of HMIC, with a new much expanded remit, a new chief inspector, and a new board. For the first time, members who did not exclusively have a police background were included as the Chief Inspector and Board members, and a new performance management regime centred on annual all-force inspections, entitled Police Effectiveness, Efficiency, and Legitimacy (PEEL), was developed between 2012 and 2015.

This 'new' HMIC was considered sufficiently successful that the Home Secretary announced the creation of a new 'independent inspectorate' for FRSs (May 2016). This later emerged in 2017 as an extended reincarnation of HMIC, renamed Her Majesty's Inspectorate of Constabulary and Fire & Rescue Services (HMICFRS).

Ironically, however, by May 2015, these changes to governance structures had resulted in potential governance and accountability arrangements in the sector as a whole becoming more complex and opaque, when the original intention was to make them more transparent (Murphy et al. 2017).

Accountability and Transparency of Police Forces

Police forces in the UK are funded through central taxation and annual grants allocated to Police Authorities and, since 2013, PCCs. They also receive local funding via local council tax precepts. Police services, therefore, need to respond to local priorities and communities in their annual policing plans. At the same time, forces are required to acknowledge and implement ministerial initiatives, and they receive a significant proportion of their funding directly from central government. In other words, as the National Audit Office (NAO 2015) acknowledged, they are accountable in different directions and to different masters.

The next section will set out the arrangements for police accountability before the 2010 election, before examining the impact of reforms introduced by the Conservative-led coalition and subsequent Conservative governments in the period since then. It will look, in particular, at how the introduction of directly elected PCCs and information 'transparency' has developed for English and Welsh police forces.

Pre-2010

In 1964, the UK government introduced *police authorities* to oversee territorial police forces. These authorities were made up of both nominated local councillors and appointed members (Jackson and Dewing 2009) and they had a statutory role to oversee the activities of each police constabulary. They were responsible for setting local policing priorities, recruiting senior officers, monitoring performance and expenditure, and ensuring that Chief Constables balanced both national and local priorities (House of Commons Home Affairs Committee 2010). Collectively, through the Association of Police Authorities, police authorities also formed a key part of national 'tripartite' arrangements that also involved the Home Office and the Association of Chief Police Officers.

These three agencies aimed to coordinate policymaking and join-up inter-agency service delivery, whilst remaining functionally autonomous. This arrangement sought to ensure that policing would not become overtly party-political because no government minister was directly in control of forces, and that professional officers were responsible for day-to-day operational duties, although concerns about the accountability of forces to local communities persisted. In practical terms, police authorities held the service to account locally, but senior officers liaised with ministers and civil servants to address more serious and organised crime that transcended the geographical territories of individual forces.

From the 1990s onwards, forces were required to report their performance against Audit Commission and central government indicators. This requirement was initiated by previous Conservative administrations and overseen by the Audit Commission. The indicators included response times to emergency calls, crime levels, detection rates, the number of officers per head of population, and total force expenditure (Audit Commission 1995, 2009). In addition, forces were subjected to 'efficiency and effectiveness' assessments from HMIC, which reported to the Home Secretary.

Between 1997 and 2010, the New Labour administrations maintained this approach and expanded the range of indicators against which police forces were assessed and included various Home Office performance and Treasury financial targets (Cabinet Office 2009). Ministers set up a new improvement body, the National Policing Improvement Agency (NPIA), together with more effective whistleblowing and complaints arrangements implemented through the (former) Independent Police Complaints Commission, which had itself replaced the former Police Complaints Authority.

During this period, inspection bodies were producing unprecedented amounts of performance information that was publicly available, annually reported and could be interrogated by freely available web-based tools and techniques. At the same time, the government provided financial support for improvements and the potential of extra freedom from central government controls and monitoring, in order to incentivise forces to perform well against their targets. Figure 5.1 (Murphy et al. 2017) illustrates how these accountability arrangements operated in practice before 2012.

THE COALITION GOVERNMENT

In 2010, the coalition administration implemented its response to the economic recession, in what would become a long term policy of 'austerity localism' (Lowndes and Pratchett 2012). This gave local public bodies more freedom to decide their own priorities, in a period when national economic policy severely restricted public expenditure. Ministers largely dismantled New Labour's performance management

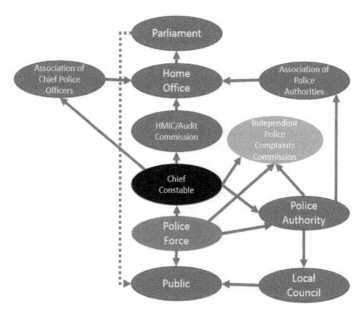

The direction of the arrow indicates who is accountable to whom

Fig. 5.1 Pre-PCC police accountability arrangements (Murphy et al. 2017)

arrangements and the improvement infrastructure that supported it. They abolished the Audit Commission and abandoned the tripartite leadership arrangements. The NPIA was replaced by a new College of Policing with significantly reduced funding although HMIC, having survived the bonfire of the quangos (*The Guardian* 2012), was accorded a new expanded and more influential role and eventually morphed into the new HMICFRS under the subsequent Conservative administration.

Following this, 2012 was a critical period and marked a turning point in the accountability and transparency regime for police services. A new chief inspector and HMIC board were appointed, with the first non-police officers appointed to hold the chief inspectors and board posts. The Home Office increased HMIC's budget in order to fund a new programme of force inspections under a new PEEL framework (HMIC 2017), which henceforth provided regular assessments of organisational performance, as well as thematic and more specialist inspections of services and individual incidents. The nature and form of the post-2012 HMIC operations gradually widened in scope and in terms of the organisations that fell under its remit, and its development and modus operandi has increasingly deployed tools and techniques originally pioneered by the Audit Commission.

Police forces are required to publish various datasets on the new www.police.uk website as a result of the *Police Reform and Social Responsibility Act 2011*. On announcing these 'transparency' initiatives, which released tranches of raw data onto public websites (Prime Minister's Office 2011), ministers argued that this would allow the public to assess the performance of their local force more easily and thus enhance accountability to local residents as a result.

In 2012, ministers also introduced elected PCCs to provide a direct and democratic link between forces and their local residents. PCCs were introduced explicitly to improve public accountability. They were a response to the lack of public awareness of police authorities and their activities (Rowe and Lister 2015). PCCs would henceforth be responsible for ensuring local policing needs are met in all forces outside London (where this task is undertaken by the elected Mayor). The legislation also meant that PCCs, in addition to being accountable locally, are partly accountable to the Home Secretary, because the legislation requires them 'to provide for the national strategic policing requirement' (Raine 2015).

In addition, other changes meant that the national 'tripartite' governance structure was replaced with a 'quadripartite' arrangement, as they also led to the creation of Police and Crime Panels (PCPs), to provide overview and scrutiny of PCCs and hold PCCs to account between elections. PCPs comprise local councillors and independent members, but (unlike the former police authorities) chief constables are not accountable to them. Additional actors, including the public, the PCC's political party (in those cases where they are not an independent), community safety partnerships, criminal justice boards and other criminal justice providers, are also now involved (see Fig. 5.2 for simplified illustration). Nonetheless, it is clear that an increasing number of organisations are involved in overseeing and delivering the police service, and it could be argued that the reforms have complicated rather than simplified the nature of police accountability (Raine 2015; Raine and Keasey 2012). Others, however, argue that the governance and leadership arrangements are currently in a transitional phase, which will be simplified in due course.

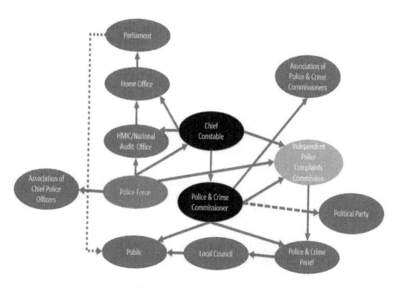

The direction of the arrow indicates who is accountable to whom

Fig. 5.2 Post 2012 PCC accountability model (Murphy et al. 2017)

In the original report to the National Audit Office, we compared the performance of the governance, delivery and assurance regime for the police against the 10 areas outlined in Chapter 1, at the time of the general elections in May 2010 and May 2015. As with the other services and for ease of presentation, the 10 evaluative criteria were presented in four groups, with the state of public assurance and the risks to value for money assessed against five risk categories.

The assessment of police services presented a conundrum. Not only does the summary presentation in Fig. 5.3, conceal much of the detail, which it does in all four services; in the case of police services, it also conceals a significant change in the direction of its performance. In the other services, the direction of travel between 2010 and 2015 was in general terms unidirectional and relatively consistent. In police services, as mentioned above, 2012 actually marked a sea change. Prior to 2012, the changes in both assurance and potential value for money risks meant that they were generally deteriorating; after 2012 they generally tended to improve, so that by 2015 they were the only one of the four services, where the evaluation found overall improvement between 2010 and 2015. In addition, some of the assessment of the 'risks' to achieving value for money were strongly influenced by several factors: the relative immaturity of the new financial reporting arrangements under the Local Audit and Accountability Act 2012; the new PEEL assessments being introduced by HMIC; the underdevelopment of the evidence base upon which these and other assessments were reliant; and the immaturity of the sectors improvement infrastructure. By 2015, these arrangements were not only improving but their rate of improvement was accelerating. Whilst, the other potential contenders for the leadership of the Conservative party (George Osborne and Boris Johnson) took higher profiles in the contemporary 'Brexit' debates, Theresa May continued to pursue the police reform agenda which was both popular in her own party and occasioned limited opposition from Labour and the Liberal Democrats and was a devolved matter in Scotland and Northern Ireland.

The *Policing and Crime Bill*, subsequently, the *Policing and Crime Act 2017*, was intended to improve cooperation between the 'blue light' services; extend freedom of information; improve public scrutiny and assurance; change the way complaints against the police are handled; and rename the Independent Complaints Commission as the Independent Office for Police Conduct with a director general appointed by the Queen.

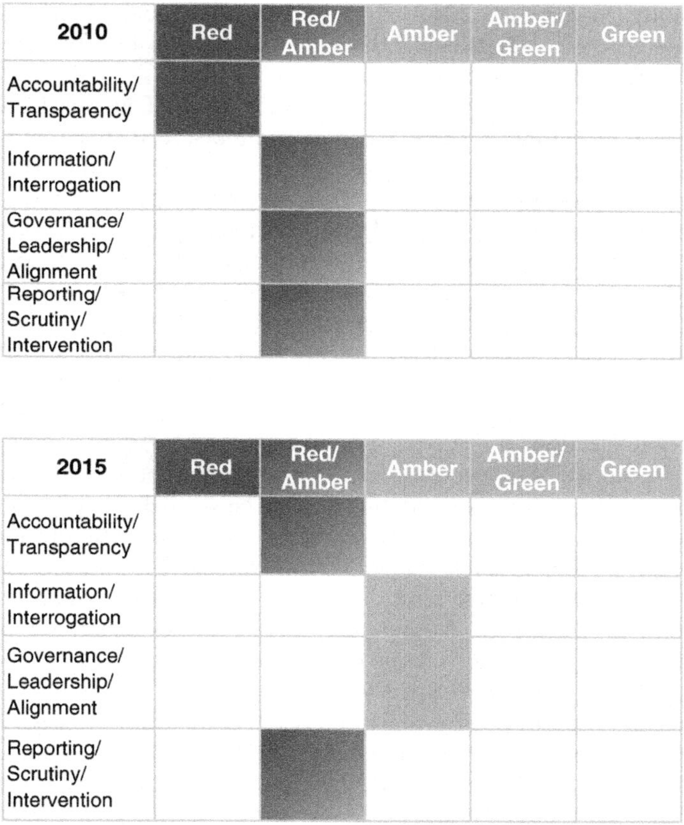

2010	Red	Red/ Amber	Amber	Amber/ Green	Green
Accountability/ Transparency	■				
Information/ Interrogation		■			
Governance/ Leadership/ Alignment		■			
Reporting/ Scrutiny/ Intervention		■			

2015	Red	Red/ Amber	Amber	Amber/ Green	Green
Accountability/ Transparency		■			
Information/ Interrogation			■		
Governance/ Leadership/ Alignment			■		
Reporting/ Scrutiny/ Intervention		■			

Fig. 5.3 Police Services: Public Assurance 2010–2015

Chapter 2 of the 2017 Act explicitly promotes and extends the role of PCCs and enables them to assume responsibility for the leadership of local FRSs. Since the act was implemented there has also been the administrative equivalent of a 'vote of confidence' in the leadership, governance, and practice of the (former) HMIC and the various PEEL performance management arrangements. The role and remit of HMIC has been extended to include responsibility for inspecting FRSs (Home Office 2017) and the proposed new arrangements for Fire Service inspections show a remarkable similarity to the PEEL police service inspections (HMICFRS 2017). In addition, the evidence and information base is to be strengthened through the creation of a website modelled on the www.police.uk website.

It is clear in retrospect that the interrogation of financial and performance information became more difficult between 2010 and 2012. This was *inter alia,* due to a reduction in research and evaluation capacity from within the Home Office and the abolition of the Audit Commission and NPIA. Similarly, at the local level, the abolition of the former police authorities led to a loss of knowledge and experience (both from elected members and analytical support staff), and the new arrangements took some time to recover these resources. For example, PCPs were made responsible for scrutinising and monitoring the performance of PCCs, but these bodies did not necessarily nor extensively draw upon the resources of the now-defunct authorities (LGA/CfPS 2011). The election of more party-politically based commissioners at the second round of PCC elections in 2016 suggests that this resource may be utilised more extensively in the future. Nevertheless, for some time there was much less capacity within the system to analyse and interpret activities in order to inform accountability. Similarly, transparency initiatives could not be effective if residents have neither the resources nor the inclination to analyse the datasets that public bodies make available—as the parallel case of English local government suggests (Eckersley et al. 2014)—and as discussed in a previous chapter.

Although the contribution from HMIC significantly increased the new arrangements for external hierarchical accountability, they remain to some extent confused and overlapping, with a number of 'agents' to whom forces should report and an unclear division of responsibilities. For example, the *Local Audit and Accountability Act 2014* gave the National Audit Office the right of access to both the Home Office and PCCs, but only HMIC can inspect police forces and make a judgement on their efficiency and effectiveness. In fact, the complex and changing organisational landscape (NAO 2014), together with the attendant accountability and transparency arrangements, at the time led the National Audit Office to raise significant concerns about the assurance of value for money in police services (NAO 2015).

There was also considerable scepticism amongst politicians and the wider policing and criminal justice community as to the value of introducing PCCs in the first place. Together with high levels of public confusion and disinterest, this scepticism culminated in turnouts of less than

15% for the first PCC elections in November 2012 (Lister and Rowe 2015). Shortly afterwards, the Independent Police Commission (established by the Home Secretary under the former Chief Commissioner of the Metropolitan Police Lord Stevens), recommended that the 'significantly flawed' model should be abandoned (Independent Police Commission 2013). When such a low percentage of residents express a preference for a PCC candidate, it raised serious questions about the legitimacy of the post and whether mechanisms such as direct elections would actually make commissioners more accountable. Although an increased percentage of voters did participate in the next round of PCC elections (in May 2016), this was undoubtedly because they were timed to coincide with elections to local councils in England and the Assembly in Wales—and even then only three English PCC contests had turnouts in excess of 30% (House of Commons 2016). Furthermore, many more of the successful candidates represented a political party compared to 2012, which complicates the accountability relationships even further in these areas (see Fig. 5.2).

Nevertheless, the success of Theresa May in the Conservative leadership contest and the increasing and overwhelming dominance of the implication of the Brexit vote, in both political debate and in legislative programming, meant that there would be no change in direction regarding the evolution of the regime that sought to monitor financial and operational performance and provide public assurance in relation to territorial police services.

There is some evidence to suggest that accountability is improving. Early studies of PCCs have found that they focused most of their efforts in building their rapport with the public, despite the fact that they were also involved in other accountability relationships within policing (Lister and Rowe 2015; Caless and Owens 2016; Murphy et al. 2017). This has paid off to some extent, as the public has become increasingly likely to correspond with PCCs, and they almost certainly have a higher public profile than former members of police authorities (Lister and Rowe 2015). Their visibility and public profile was of course enhanced by the debate and subsequent role afforded to them (and HMIC) by the *Policing and Crime Act 2017*, in terms of their potential responsibility for FRSs. HMIC's role and responsibilities, notwithstanding the FRSs, has continued to expand since the 2015 general election and its assessments have become more sophisticated. The evidence base has also started to improve and, to some extent, become more transparent.

EVALUATION OF ACCOUNTABILITY

In Chapter 2 we argued that to fully embrace a model of accountability that is effective in critiquing public services, we need to understand accountability as having both individual and systemic natures. At the level of the individual, in addition to the improved organisational transparency occasioned by the election of PCCs, the HMIC assessments, and improvements in the evidence and information available to the public, there is also the direct experience of the individual complaints against the police. Whilst, there is no doubt that the Independent Police Complaints Commission, and the internal police complaints arrangements that it oversaw, were a huge improvement on the previous Police Complaints Authority, it is too early to assess whether the Independent Office for Police Conduct introduced by the 2017 Act will improve individual accountability and transparency in the police.

In addition, public services (and individuals within those services) are subject to scrutiny, overview, inspection, and direction from external sources. From an organisational perspective, in Chapter 2 we drew attention to four questions or issues.

- What are the governance mechanisms in place to provide leadership management and crucially internal scrutiny and oversight?
- What level of local discretion exists in how the service is configured and delivered, and what are the things it must deliver?
- What external regulation or inspection is there—and does this contribute to public assurance, service improvement, and organisational development?
- What are the funding mechanisms, and what balance of central/ local funding exists?

We suggested that political accountability, from local service institutions to (political) central government, from central government to the electorate, and from local service institutions to the local electorate, is essential for overall accountability. Political accountability is the knowledge that, at some point, decision-makers will be held accountable at the ballot box for the impact of their decisions. We also contend, however, that this is a necessary but insufficient component to facilitate accountability, particularly at the operational level.

The governance, strategic and operational arrangements that have developed since 2012, on the whole, appear to have provided clearer and improved leadership and management for police services at the national and local level. However, whilst external scrutiny via PCCs and HMICFRS has improved, it is less certain whether internal scrutiny and oversight via PCPs has improved or is adequate. In the period since 2012, despite tight financial restrictions, external regulation and inspection has matured and developed, and improved its contribution to public assurance, service delivery, and organisational development in the police service.

However, the total resources available to the service continue to reduce and has inevitably limited local discretion in how the service is configured and delivered. There is increasing evidence to show that the long-term and effective prevention and protection services are being disproportionately and adversely affected and the National Audit Office are currently investigating the financial sustainability of police forces. Nevertheless, the government clearly considers that the sector has lessons for the other public services they are looking to reform.

CONCLUSIONS

Overall the new arrangements for policing in England and Wales have improved governance, accountability, transparency and operational delivery of the service, although there is clear potential for further improvement. The current arrangements are more robust, albeit more complex, than their immediate predecessors. As a consequence of the imposition of PCCs, they are becoming more responsive to communities than the police authorities they replaced. Despite the abolition of centralised targeting frameworks, the new PEEL programme and the continued power of the Home Secretary (either directly or via HMICFRS) to intervene in the governance and management of forces mean that strong accountability structures are available, although the level of independence afforded the HMICFRS is limited.

Because there are more actors involved in the organisational landscape of policing and the relative newness of accountability arrangements, it is not always clear how roles and responsibilities are distributed across this landscape. As a result, there is a risk that the public does not have a clear understanding of roles and responsibilities under the new arrangements, which makes it more difficult for them (and the statutory bodies) to hold officials to account for their actions. One area, for instance, that would benefit from development is the internal and external scrutiny and overview provided by PCPs. The potential additional responsibilities for FRSs, the uncertain financial outlook, and the further diversity in governance and accountability arrangements will increase the need to address this challenge.

REFERENCES

Audit Commission. (1995). *Local Authority Performance Indicators 1994/5: Volume 3 Police and Fire Services.* London.

Audit Commission. (2009). *Use of Resources Framework—Overall Approach and Key Lines of Enquiry 2008* (as updated in February 2009). London: Audit Commission.

Cabinet Office. (2009). *Public Service Agreements.* London.

Caless, B., & Owens, J. (2016). *Police and Crime Commissioners: The Transformation of Police Accountability.* Bristol: Policy Press.

Eckersley, P., Ferry, L., & Zakaria, Z. (2014). A 'Panoptical' or 'Synoptical' Approach to Monitoring Performance? Local Public Services in England and the Widening Accountability Gap. *Critical Perspectives on Accounting, 25*(6), 529–538.

The Guardian. (2012, August 22). Bonfire of the Quangos: The Victims. *The Guardian.* Retrieved August 22, 2012, from http://www.theguardian.com/politics/2012/aug/22/bonfire-quangos-victims-list.

HMIC. (2017). *State of Policing: The Annual Assessment of Policing in England and Wales, 2016.* London: Her Majesty's Inspectorate of Constabulary.

HMICFRS. (2017). *Proposed Fire and Rescue Services Inspection Programme and Framework 2018/19. For Consultation.* London: Her Majesty's Inspectorate of Constabulary and Fire and Rescue Services.

Home Office. (2017). *Fire and Rescue National Framework for England Government Consultation.* London.

House of Commons. (2016). *Police and Crime Commissioner Elections: 2016.* London.

House of Commons Home Affairs Committee. (2010). *Policing: Police and Crime Commissioners. Second Report of Session 2010–11.* London.

Independent Police Commission. (2013). *Policing for a Better Britain.* London.

Jackson, C., & Dewing, I. P. (2009). Police Authorities in England and Wales: Board Composition and Corporate Governance. *Public Money Manage, 29*(5), 292–298.

Lewis, B. (2017). *Fire Minister's Speech to Reform.* London: Home Office.

LGA/CfPS. (2011). *Police and Crime Panels Guidance on Role and Composition.* London: Local Government Association/Centre for Public Scrutiny.

Lister, S., & Rowe, M. (2015). Electing Police and Crime Commissioners in England and Wales: Prospecting for the Democratisation of Policing. *Policing and Society, 25*(4), 358–377.

Lowndes, V., & Pratchett, L. (2012). Local Governance Under the Coalition Government: Austerity, Localism and the 'Big Society'. *Local Government Studies, 38*(1), 21–40.

May, T. (2016). *Home Secretary Speech on Fire Reform.* London: Home Office.

Murphy, P., Eckersley, P., & Ferry, L. (2017). Accountability and Transparency: Police Forces in England and Wales. *Public Policy and Administration, 32*(3), 197–213.

NAO. (2014). *Police Accountability: Landscape Review.* London: National Audit Office.

NAO. (2015). *Financial Sustainability of Police Forces in England and Wales.* London.

Prime Minister's Office. (2011). *Letter to Cabinet Ministers on Transparency and Open Data.* Prime Minister's Office.

Raine, J. W. (2015). Enhancing Police Accountability in England and Wales: What Differences Are Police and Crime Commissioners Making? In *Police Services* (pp. 97–113). Berlin: Springer.

Raine, J. W., & Keasey, P. (2012). From Police Authorities to Police and Crime Commissioners: Might Policing Become More Publicly Accountable? *International Journal of Emergency Services, 1*(2), 122–134.

Rowe, M., & Lister, S. (2015). Accountability of Policing. In *Accountability of Policing* (pp. 17–33). London: Routledge.

CHAPTER 6

Fire and Rescue

Peter Murphy, Kirsten Greenhalgh, Laurence Ferry, and
Russ Glennon

Abstract The supposed 'success' of Theresa May's police reform has justified the 'model' for recent reform of the Fire and Rescue Services. Fire and Rescue Services entered the period of the coalition government on an improving and accelerating service delivery trajectory, albeit still trailing the other services. The coalition government's 'austerity localism'; aligned to financial constraints turned this direction of travel on its' head. By 2015 and 2016, both the NAO and PAC were demanding significant regime change in the service. Since 2015, there have been improvements to accountability and transparency, (it would be difficult not to act and act decisively, given the inadequacy of previous arrangements). More recently differences between promises and implementation, ambitions, and delivery are beginning to appear.

Keywords Fire and rescue · Reform · Accountability · Governance
Police fire and crime commissioners

Introduction

The government is in the process of enacting reforms to the fire and rescue services (FRSs) modelled on the policing reforms (referred to in Chapter 5 of this book) via provisions in the *Crime and Policing Act 2017*, which received royal assent in January 2018. The FRSs have, like all public services, experienced austerity localism (Lowndes

© The Author(s) 2019
P. Murphy et al., *Public Service Accountability*,
https://doi.org/10.1007/978-3-319-93384-9_6

and Pratchett 2012) and a performance management, governance, and assurance regime similar to the one imposed on local government. This has recently been deemed inadequate and in need of urgent and extensive reform (Lewis 2017; May 2016). Unlike the other services, major reforms in FRSs can be anticipated in the future rather than experienced during 2010–2015. This chapter will nevertheless use our evaluative framework to describe the implications for FRSs.

This chapter will first focus on the changes in governance, accountability, and public assurance arrangements for FRSs in the years between 2010 and 2015 which resulted from long-term austerity and uncertainty within UK public services. It will then move on to focus on how recent national government reforms have changed the nature of accountability arrangements. The chapter begins by providing some background to the economic and political landscape with a chronology of events and then moves on to discuss the public assurance, accountability, and transparency arrangements.

Political and Economic Landscape

The outcome of the 2010 general election, a hung parliament, resulted in a coalition between the Conservative and Liberal Democrat parties. The UK had been suffering from the impact of the global financial crisis, beginning in the USA in December 2007, with the recession officially starting in the second quarter of 2008.

In spite of the recession, the FRS annual budget for 2009/2010 was the second of three relatively generous financial settlements from the government. However, the government, the Audit Commission, the Local Government Association (LGA) and the Society of Local Authority Chief Executives (SOLACE) were all advocating prudence for local authorities in their short- and long-term budgetary planning. Local government authorities and fire and rescue authorities (FRAs) had therefore been preparing for significant reductions in future financial settlements for some time before the axe finally fell. The three main responses from local government and FRAs between 2008 and 2010 were to change priorities, cut expenditure, or build up reserves; in many cases all three responses were employed (Audit Commission 2008, 2009, 2010; Ferry and Eckersley 2011, 2012, 2015; Lowndes and McCaughie 2013). By the time the coalition government came into power both the FRSs and their local authority colleagues had, in terms of service delivery and financial management, become very robust and resilient organisations (Walker 2015; Jones 2017).

In June 2010 the new chancellor, George Osborne, delivered his emergency budget and his 'accelerated plan to reduce the deficit'. The intention was to reduce the 'long-term structural deficit' within the length of the parliamentary term, with 80% of savings being derived from public expenditure reductions and 20% from increased growth. This was one of many economic and social targets that the coalition government failed to achieve and led to even more stringent targets for locally delivered public services. FRAs started the 2014/2015 financial year with, on average, 33% less in government funding than four years earlier and with predictions of a further 10% cut in the 2015/2016 financial year (LGA 2014).

Contextually, it needs to be noted that there was a radical shift in policy between the previous administration, which had invested more in public services, and the coalition's economic policies and their significant reductions in public funding. At the same time the devolution agenda, which transferred powers to Scotland and Wales, resulted in diversification of both organisation and service delivery within FRSs across the UK. In Scotland, the governance and structure of the service changed radically with the merger of 8 FRSs into one single service whilst in England these remained relatively untouched. However, accountability, performance management, the services' collaboration with service delivery partners and human resource management issues all changed and became more complex.

THE CHRONOLOGY OF EVENTS

In his speech at the Harrogate Fire Conference in June 2010, after just over a month of the coalition government administration, the new Fire Minister, Bob Neill, claimed that there was 'significant scope to find efficiencies in the way FRSs operate', and that an 'overly bureaucratic system' had developed with 'too much central government prescription' based on national standards and targets. He therefore challenged the service, collectively, to take responsibility for the sector, and join him in a 'strategic review' of the sector and the national framework (Murphy and Greenhalgh 2011a). He acknowledged that the government would have to provide assurance about responding to national emergencies and the adequacy of national and local emergency resilience arrangements but expected FRSs to deliver 'more for less'. In return, there was a promise of greater financial autonomy and the abandonment of national diversity targets and national guidance on recruitment and development (Neill 2010).

Significant changes were revealed almost immediately. The Chancellor unveiled his plans to curb public spending and the so-called 'bonfire of the QUANGOs' (*The Guardian* 2012), abolishing over a hundred non-departmental public bodies, as part of his emergency budget. The Secretary of State for Communities and Local Government, Eric Pickles, announced plans to abolish the Audit Commission and terminate Comprehensive Area Assessments (CAA), Local Area Agreements (LAA), the National Indicator Set and the 'era of top-down government' (Pickles 2010a, b). However, the emphasis on prevention, protection and community safety, and the requirement for Integrated Risk Management Planning would remain.

As a response to the planned abolition of the Audit Commission and its role to 'protect the public purse', the Local Government Association were promoting sector-led improvement and regulation as a replacement for CAA as suggested within the LGA publication, *Taking the Lead* (2011a). In December 2010, four *Fire Futures* reports were published as a result of a wide-ranging sector-led independent review identifying, 'a series of options for the future of fire and rescue provision in England' (Ministry of Housing 2011). These reports addressed the fire sectors role, efficiency, accountability, and work with other emergency services but were rejected. The government's response to the *Fire Futures* reports was to say that it did not intend to control and direct the way in which FRSs were delivered but would support options which aligned with its emerging policy for public sector reform and the localism agenda.

Whilst the official select committee report on the abolition of the Audit Commission was not published until July 2011, the announcement of plans to abolish the commission in August 2010 by Eric Pickles pre-dated this report by almost a year. Unsurprisingly the vast majority of Audit Commission staff quickly found alternative employment and the Select Committee acknowledged the subsequent inevitability of the commission's abolition by the time of its report, with the formal closure taking place on 31 March 2015. However, the select committee nevertheless asked its witnesses whether they supported the abolition. It is interesting to note that Peter Holland (then Chief Fire Officer of Lancashire FRA) responded on behalf of the Chief Fire Officers Association (CFOA), saying that whilst there were caveats, the commission had on balance been beneficial to the service and should be retained and reformed, rather than abolished (House of Commons Communities and Local Government Committee 2011).

Shortly after this, the coalition government's proposals for public sector reform and the ambition to ensure 'everyone had access to the best public services' were published in The *Open Public Services White Paper*(Cabinet Office 2011) on 1 July 2011 with the declaration that, 'the old, centralised approach to public service delivery is broken'. There was recognition of the difference between public services and that a one-size-fits-all policy would be inappropriate. The white paper therefore drew a distinction between three types of public services and the governments' intentions towards them: individual or personal services used by people on an individual basis; neighbourhood services defined as being provided very locally on a collective rather than an individual basis; and commissioned services—whether by central or local government—that cannot be devolved to communities or individuals.

Whilst the FRSs are not specifically mentioned in the white paper, the fourth national framework (DCLG 2012) that followed made it clear that FRSs were henceforth to be treated as commissioned services, with the FRA being the commissioning authority. In addition to the separation of commissioners and providers, there would also be open commissioning and credible independent accreditation of providers to ensure accreditation of what works. Clear mechanisms of accountability were required to ensure that:

> [C]ommissioners are held to account by users and citizens for creating choice and choosing providers who offer high-quality, cost-effective services; and, secondly, that providers are held to account by commissioners and service users. (Cabinet Office 2011)

The accountability of providers would be managed through a combination of mutually reinforcing choice (alternative providers within the marketplace), user engagement or 'voice', and transparency mechanisms (the public as 'armchair auditors' furnished with more publicly available data and information). External audit and inspection would also be employed to ensure that relevant standards are met and the commissioners and provider have the necessary financial controls in place.

In a busy year for the Communities Secretary, he also announced the closure of the Government Regional Offices (DCLG 2010), formerly the hosts of Regional Resilience Forums, established by the *Civil Contingencies Act 2004*. These regional offices compiled and reviewed regional risk registers, co-ordinated Local Resilience Forums and community risk registers, and linked with national resilience arrangements, including the national risk assessment (Cabinet Office 2015) particularly at times of national or widespread emergencies. The loss of this key part of the infrastructure was particularly exposed in the winter floods of 2013–2014 (Murphy 2015b), and by the outbreaks of avian influenza ('bird flu') in February 2015.

In the period between the 2010 general election and July 2012, the rhetoric of austerity was pervasive throughout public services, including FRSs. The aims to reduce the size of the state and the structural deficit resulted in proposals for severe reductions in public expenditure accompanied by the introduction of market mechanisms to reform public services. The DCLG, under Eric Pickles, was, as one would expect, a zealous implementer of these policy changes and all services within the department's portfolio suffered the consequences.

The 2012 National Framework and the Knight Review

As mentioned above the fourth National Framework for FRSs was published in 2012 with an open-ended duration. In his ministerial foreword, Bob Neill stated it would:

> Continue to provide an overall strategic direction to FRAs, but will not seek to tell them how they should serve their communities. They are free to operate in a way that enables the most efficient delivery of their services. … Ultimately, it is to local communities, not Government, that FRAs are accountable. (DCLG 2012)

He 'acknowledged the proficiency and experience of FRAs' and allowed them 'freedom and flexibility to deliver the services for which they are respected and renowned without being hampered by Whitehall bureaucracy and red tape' (DCLG 2012).

The 2012 Framework was addressed exclusively to the Commissioners of the service, the FRAs. Its remit was restricted to England, following administrative devolution in Scotland, Wales, and Northern Ireland.

In an attempt to avoid overstepping boundaries following devolution, any reference within the framework to responsibilities arising from the Civil Contingencies Act 2004 was referred to as 'national' roles and responsibilities of both the government and the FRSs. Ironically there was a lack of clarity in these 'national' roles.

NEW ARRANGEMENTS FOR DELIVERY, PERFORMANCE AND PUBLIC ASSURANCE

The abolition of the Audit Commission and its performance frameworks, and the introduction of sector-led improvement, moved the performance management of public bodies from a panoptical to a synoptical approach (Eckersley et al. 2014). This comprised sector-led improvement and a new regulatory system, with public sector bodies responsible for their own performance and accountability at the local not national level (LGA 2011b). This new approach required both local government and the fire and rescue sector to take a greater role in their own regulation and performance in order to improve public assurance, accountability, and transparency, with transparency at the fore (Cabinet Office 2011).

New public assurance, accountability, and transparency arrangements were introduced to support the government's public service reform plan (Cabinet Office 2011) and arrangements for commissioned services delivered under the 2012 National Framework. Throughout this period the Department of Communities and Local Government retained responsibility for FRSs.

As stated in Chapter 1, the original National Audit Office report (Ferry and Murphy 2015), from which this book emerged, examined ten related concepts in terms of their application to the overarching process of accountability. That analysis corralled these concepts into four groups and compared the 'state of play' in May 2015 with the situation in May 2010. The analysis produced indications of the quality, quantity, scope, and maturity of the prevailing arrangements for public and stakeholder assurance. However, whilst each of these areas provides a piece of the jigsaw puzzle, it is only when they are viewed as a whole that a more comprehensive overall judgement of accountability and public assurance can be made.

ACCOUNTABILITY AND TRANSPARENCY

The Secretary of State for Communities and Local Government was accountable to Parliament for the overall stewardship of FRSs whilst the accountability for the stewardship of the resources allocated to the (then) 46 FRAs and the Permanent Secretary to the DCLG oversaw providing assurance that grants are properly accounted for, and ensuring regularity, propriety, and value for money.

The fourth Fire and Rescue National Framework for England (DCLG 2012) defined the roles and responsibilities of local FRAs with each individual FRAs overseeing the policy and service delivery of a FRS. The day-to-day command of the FRS was the responsibility of the chief fire officer (CFO) who was accountable to the FRA. Funding came from business rates, a levy on council tax, and fees and charges from services provided, such as training, through the Local Government Departmental Expenditure Limit. Financial controls included clear responsibilities around expenditure, financial duties and rules for prudence in spending, internal checks for compliance, and external checks by an independent auditor.

The Local Authority (Executive Arrangements) (Meetings and Access to Information) (England) Regulations 2012, which also apply to FRAs, were intended to introduce greater transparency and openness into council and authority meetings. Members of the public can only be refused admission in limited circumstances and they must be able to access documents that relate to meetings and executive decisions. In addition, an FRS is required to make a range of datasets available to the public in accordance with the DCLG's *Code of Recommended Practice on Data Transparency* (more often known as the *Local Government Transparency Code* 2014), including, *inter alia*, publication of annual accounts, senior employee salaries, councillor allowances and expenses, copies of contracts and tenders, and grants to the voluntary and social enterprise sectors. It must also make available policies, performance and external audit, and details key inspections and indicators on fiscal and financial position.

Since 2010, the FRS performance management regime, including arrangements for assessing value for money, have been focused around the LGA sector-led improvement approach (see chapter 3). As a result of mounting concerns about the adequacy of this approach, the NAO undertook both a Local Government study, and a Value for Money study (NAO 2015a, b) which were followed by a Public Accounts Committee report (House of Commons Public Accounts Committee 2016b). These all identified 'gaps in this localised system' and demonstrated significant inadequacies in financial and performance management, value for money and public assurance. They also led to calls for the restitution of an independent fire service inspectorate (Murphy and Greenhalgh 2014). The previous inspectorate had been replaced by the Audit Commission and then subsequently a 'chief fire service advisor' within DCLG, this inspection responsibility was then transferred to a civil servant, subject to the civil service code and answerable to the department before then transferring to the Home Office in 2016.

The NAO report and subsequent calls for the restitution of an independent inspectorate implicitly acknowledge the oversimplification of the relationship between accountability and transparency, claimed by the then Secretary of State, Eric Pickles, i.e. that greater transparency was the same as greater accountability[1] or that losses of accountability where adequately compensated for through improvements in transparency. In earlier chapters, we have built upon Hood's (2010) seminal paper, and its application to public services (Ferry et al. 2015), as a means to demonstrate that the relationship between accountability and transparency is complex, overlapping, and situationally dependent and that each can exist separately to each other in both theoretical and practical senses. The NAO and Public Accounts Committee reports clearly show that by 2015 the contemporary arrangements for both accountability and transparency in FRSs had become unacceptable.

EVIDENCE, INFORMATION, AND ANALYSIS

The availability, analysis, and transparency of data, and particularly performance data, by independent researchers/armchair auditors had also become increasingly difficult after 2010 (Ferry and Murphy 2015). Previously, the Audit Commission collected and published national performance statistics, making them publicly available on interactive websites. The abolition of the Commission resulted in national reports being made available through the National Archives. However, no other data

---

[1] This statement from the Secretary of State is no longer available and was later corrected and 'updated' on the governments websites on 8th May 2015 (DCLG 2015a).

or information, including local reports were transferred, and no other central repository was established or used. The proposal by the coalition government to outsource the collection, analysis, and reporting of the government's fire service statistics by the DCLG (2015b) has yet to be implemented. The governments fire statistics, together with financial and performance databases from CFOA and CIPFA, do allow for investigation and analysis of expenditure and some performance information, but the latter two were only available by subscription. Furthermore, the fire peer challenge and operational assessment commissioned by all 46 FRSs in England and Wales, or the fire authorities' response to the assessments were initially published on the LGA website but were withdrawn by the LGA in 2015 and only a minority are available on fire authority websites.

Consequently, since the Audit Commission's abolition, there has been a significant loss in audit capacity only partially compensated for by the operational research at the NAO. The historical paucity of independent academic research capacity in the management of fire and rescue relative to other services compounded this lack of independent scrutiny (Wankhade and Murphy 2012).

Governance, Leadership, and Strategic Alignment

The *Bain report* (Bain et al. 2002) identified the 'lack of leadership throughout the service at the political, institutional and operational levels'. Between 2003 and 2010, central and local government, local FRSs Chief Officers, and the Audit Commission sought to re-establish collective sector leadership and to facilitate performance improvement, innovation, and service delivery. The *Fire and Rescue Act 2004* and the *Civil Contingencies Act 2004* prompted a period of gradual acceptance of and engagement with increasing strategic alignment through joined up policy and delivery, improved performance management, and investment in infrastructure and system support. The development of tools, techniques, systems, and interventions were behind developments in the equivalent health and local government regimes, but were rapidly progressing and generally considered to be ahead of FRSs worldwide (Murphy and Greenhalgh 2018).

Since 2010 this collective leadership has fragmented, with significant loss of capacity and coherence, accompanied by a loss of collective vision thereby compromising strategic alignment (Ferry and Murphy 2015; NAO 2015a, b). The coalition government significantly reduced its own role with the fourth National Framework proposing a 'hands off', light touch and self-governing model for local FRAs and for the support and intervention regime. As in previous periods of FRS history (Raynsford 2016), leadership and collective responsibility had largely been left to CFOA, and there emerged a clear risk to individual and collective aspirations for efficiency and value for money (Knight 2013; Murphy 2015a; NAO 2015a). Under the coalition government, FRSs and FRAs were driven, in both theory and practice, by short-term cutback management.

Fire Services respond to short and long-term emergencies with the other blue light services on a day-to-day basis. The FRA's role is to finance and equip the response to incidents and emergencies, and to enable the service to collaborate and deliver strategic and operational efficiencies. In general, the emergency services already had mature, efficient and effective cross-organisational emergency planning, resilience and interoperability capability at an operational response level. This has improved continually since modern emergency services were established after the Second World War but particularly after a series of major emergencies and disasters in the 1980s and 1990s that included the Bradford and Kings Cross fires. National interoperability has similarly improved since the *Civil Contingencies Act in 2004*, as major emergencies have become more numerous, complex and diversified. Paradoxically, regional emergency planning, regional intelligence and co-ordination and response capacity was actually reduced when the government abolished regional resilience forums and regional government officers in 2012.

REPORTING, SCRUTINY, AND INTERVENTION

Strategic advice and guidance to ministers, civil servants and fire authorities on structure, organisation and performance were provided by the chief fire service adviser in the DCLG. The annual financial reporting mandated through the *Local Audit and Accountability Act 2014*, together with statistical returns to parliament, the secretary of state and other regulators or agencies, were the only reporting requirements for individual FRSs.

The differentiated responsibilities of FRAs and FRSs that arose from the commissioner/provider split and scrutiny arrangements following the open public services white paper and the 2012 Framework were largely exercised at the local level through local government structures, regulations, and practices. However, there is no demonstrable evidence that this change made any significant impact in practice, and no discernible impact on either the amount or quality of scrutiny by FRAs. Inter-agency and collaborative working arrangements are to an extent 'horizontally' scrutinised in local resilience forums but these are relatively recent and therefore untested in their 'scrutiny' role.

FRSs are able to benchmark expenditure and budgeting through CIPFA's interactive financial database and its interrogative tools. However, in terms of external scrutiny, FRAs and FRSs had considerable discretion to determine what is reported to the public. Their reports and the data behind them are variable and provide little opportunity for meaningful comparisons across organisations, as Murphy and Greenhalgh found in a previous survey for Nottinghamshire FRS and more recently in the report for the NAO (2015b).

FRAs and FRSs were still subject to the duty of Best Value, and the secretary of state had broad intervention powers delivered through the *Local Government Act 1999* and the *Fire and Rescue Services Act 2004*. Within these acts are powers to obtain information or to take action in any circumstances where central government may wish to have an investigation or assessment. This could include a major fire incident investigation or where serious concerns exist regarding the discharging of functions or even corporate failure. The Secretary of State is required to have regard to the updated *Protocol on government intervention action on FRAs in England* (DCLG 2013) although this has not been used to date.

ASSESSMENT OF ACCOUNTABILITY ARRANGEMENTS 2010–2015

In the report commissioned by the NAO, Ferry and Murphy (2015) assessed the quality and effectiveness of accountability and public assurance provided across locally delivered services. They found that in FRSs, accountability and transparency were generally poorer in 2015 than in 2010. The performance management regime was fragmenting, the evidence base was diminishing and the improvement infrastructure and support available to fire services had suffered significant losses in both capacity and capability. In addition, major capital funding arrangements remained inflexible and expensive, and financial and resource planning was generally short-term and compliance dominated. As Knight (2013) had found earlier, and the NAO came to suspect (NAO 2015a, b), potential inter-agency efficiency gains were not being captured, still less maximised.

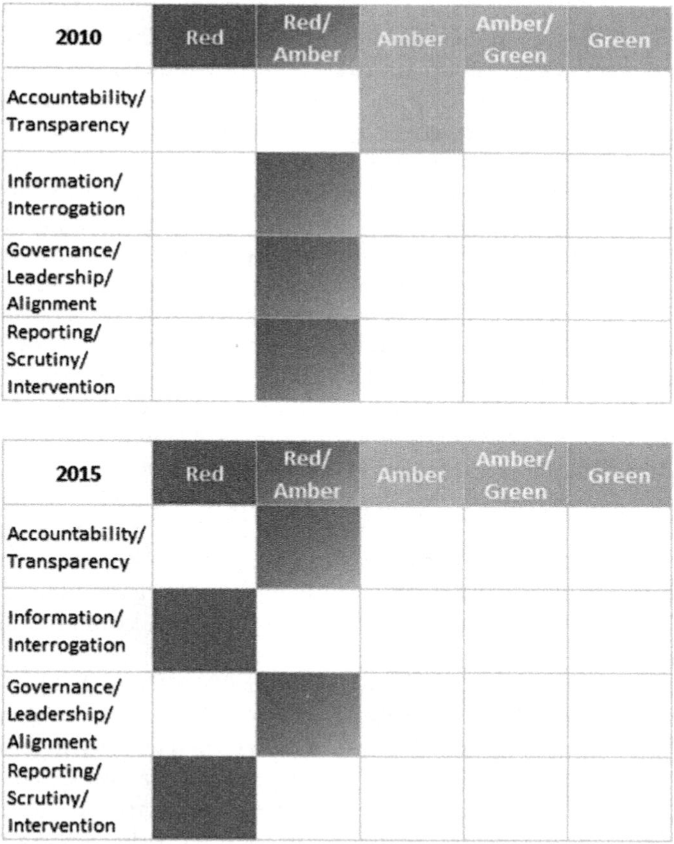

2010	Red	Red/Amber	Amber	Amber/Green	Green
Accountability/Transparency			▨		
Information/Interrogation		▨			
Governance/Leadership/Alignment		▨			
Reporting/Scrutiny/Intervention		▨			

2015	Red	Red/Amber	Amber	Amber/Green	Green
Accountability/Transparency		▨			
Information/Interrogation	▨				
Governance/Leadership/Alignment		▨			
Reporting/Scrutiny/Intervention	▨				

Fig. 6.1   Fire and rescue services: Public Assurance 2010–2015

To illustrate the historical and sectoral changes and the relative positions of the various services, Ferry and Murphy (2015) produced a series of diagrams that showed the level of public assurance and the likely risk to achieving value for money. The position for fire and rescue is shown as Fig. 6.1. The green rating represented best available practice plus known achievable potential improvements as existing in 2010, and the red represented unacceptable or poor performance. Whilst fire services had been a relatively poorly performing sector prior to the *Fire and Rescue Services*

Act 2004 and the performance assessment regimes of New Labour, it had started to improve, initially between 2004 and 2005, and at a rapidly accelerating rate from 2006 to 2010 (Murphy and Greenhalgh 2018). Unfortunately, between 2010 and 2015 this trend reversed, and the picture deteriorated to the extent shown in Fig. 6.1 at 2015.

The NAO inherited responsibility for oversight in April 2015 after formal closure of the Audit Commission on 31 March. By 5 November 2015, (ironically 'Bonfire Night[2]' in the UK—a high-pressure date for FRS), the NAO had investigated and published their report on the financial sustainability of the FRSs. This contained some searing criticisms of the contemporary performance of the service and the state of public assurance. Most criticism was levelled at the government and the DCLG in particular for its inadequate leadership and oversight of the service. The DCLG was criticised for the inadequacy of its evidence and failing to test or challenge the effectiveness of the local systems to which it has delegated accountability, regulation and oversight.

On 5th January 2016, the Prime Minister confirmed that ministerial responsibility for fire and rescue policy would transfer from DCLG back to the Home Office from whence it came in 2001. This was even before the Public Accounts Committee's subsequent investigation based on the initial NAO report (House of Commons Public Accounts Committee 2016a).

In her last speech as Home Secretary in 2016 (May 2016), Theresa May referred to a *'fire and rescue landscape still beset by poor governance and structures'* and a *'service that requires further reform to improve accountability, bring independent scrutiny and drive transparency'*. She announced that she would be tabling amendments to the *Policing and Crime Bill*, which was then part way through its parliamentary process, in order to strengthen the inspection powers that were to be included in the *Fire and Rescue Services Act 2004*. This would introduce a rigorous and independent inspectorate regime, improve collaboration between the blue light services, and improve standards and the evidence base on which local and national decisions were taken.

As we reported in Chapter 5, the creation of this 'rigorous and independent inspectorate regime' for FRSs soon became 'an extended

---

[2] Bonfire night is the annual celebration characterised by bonfires and fireworks on the 5th November aka Guy Fawkes night. Guy Fawkes was a member of the Gunpowder Plot who attempted (unsuccesfully) to blow up the Houses of Parliament in 1605.

reincarnation of HMIC renamed Her Majesty's Inspectorate of Constabulary and Fire & Rescue Services (HMICFRS)' reporting to the Home Office and taking directions from ministers. In fact, the proposed new arrangements show remarkable similarities to the PEEL police service inspections regime (HMICFRS 2017; Murphy et al. 2018). Similarly, the government's proposal for the improvement in data and information services for FRSs, is to establish a website similar to *www.police.uk*, thus helping the public 'to assess the performance of their local service...and...unleash armchair auditors to scrutinise and do their work on how their service is operating' (Home Office 2017), despite the apparent lack of evidence that this had worked for the police, or indeed local government.

The other fundamental issue for governance, accountability, and assurance from the 2017 act is the promotion of the role of police and crime commissioners (PCC). This enables PCCs to assume responsibility for local FRSs and become police, fire, and crime commissioners (PFCC). The role was enhanced on the basis of the assumed benefits that have accrued to police services. As an election manifesto commitment and a personal initiative of the prime minister, the government clearly expected this initiative to be widely adopted and enthusiastically embraced. At the time of writing only one PFCC has been approved, to take over the previously troubled Essex FRA, although there are six more applications pending on the home secretary's desk.

CONCLUSIONS

As with police services, since 2015 there have been clear improvements to accountability and transparency in FRSs, although it would be difficult not to act and act decisively given the inadequacy of previous arrangements and the coruscating reports from the NAO and the PAC. Depending on the impact of the PFCCs and the new inspectorate, together with related proposals for information management, there may be further improvements as a result of the reports. Whether this will amount to the level of comprehensive and sophisticated accountability and assurance that the public have a right to expect of emergency services facing ever more complex challenges is too early to say. The DCLG allowed oversight and assurance of the service to fall into such a parlous state, that once the government was confronted with the problem it had to act. However, the scale of operational efficiencies and the risks to the public highlighted by the NAO are still unclear; the government itself acknowledged that this could not be effectively measured by the previous system. Finally, there is the issue of continued disinvestment in the service as further reductions in public expenditure are planned up until 2021. As the Grenfell Tower disaster has shown (Hackitt 2017) FRSs are facing rapidly changing and ever more complex challenges, and they are trying to do so within a planned resource envelope that is diminishing.

REFERENCES

Audit Commission. (2008). *Crunch Time? The Impact of the Economic Downturn on Local Government Finances*. London.

Audit Commission. (2009). *When It Comes to the Crunch: How Councils Are Responding to the Recession*. London.

Audit Commission. (2010). *Surviving the Crunch: Local Finances in the Recession and Beyond*. London.

Bain, G., Lyons, M., & Young, M. (2002). *The Future of the Fire Service; Reducing Risk, Saving Lives: The Independent Review of the Fire Service*. London: TSO.

Cabinet Office. (2011). *Open Public Services (White Paper)*. London: TSO.

Cabinet Office. (2015). *National Risk Register of Civil Emergencies 2015 Edition*. London: TSO.

DCLG. (2010). *Pickles Outlines Plans to Abolish Regional Government*. London: Department for Communities and Local Government.

DCLG. (2012). *Fire and Rescue National Framework for England*. London: TSO.

DCLG. (2013). *Protocol on Government Intervention Action on Fire and Rescue Authorities in England*. London: Department for Communities and Local Government.

DCLG. (2015a). *2010 to 2015 Government Policy: Local Council Transparency and Accountability*. Policy Paper. London: Department for Communities and Local Government.

DCLG. (2015b). *Fire and Rescue Operational Statistics Bulletin for England: 2014–2015*. London: TSO.

Eckersley, P., Ferry, L., & Zakaria, Z. (2014). A 'Panoptical' or 'Synoptical' Approach to Monitoring Performance? Local Public Services in England and the Widening Accountability Gap. *Critical Perspectives on Accounting, 25*(6), 529–538.

Ferry, L., & Eckersley, P. M. (2011). Budgeting and Governing for Deficit Reduction in the UK Public Sector: Act One 'the Comprehensive Spending Review.' *Journal of Finance and Management in Public Services*, 14–23.

Ferry, L., & Eckersley, P. (2012). Budgeting and Governing for Deficit Reduction in the UK Public Sector: Act 2 'the Annual Budget.' *Public Money Manage 32*(2), 119–126.

Ferry, L., & Eckersley, P. (2015). Budgeting and Governing for Deficit Reduction in the UK Public Sector: Act Three 'Accountability and Audit Arrangements'. *Public Money Manage, 35*(3), 203–210.

Ferry, L., & Murphy, P. (2015). *Financial Sustainability, Accountability and Transparency Across Local Public Service Bodies in England Under Austerity.* Report to National Audit Office (NAO). London: National Audit Office.

Ferry, L., Eckersley, P., & Zakaria, Z. (2015). Accountability and Transparency in English Local Government: Moving from 'Matching Parts' to 'Awkward Couple?' *Financial Accountability & Management, 31*(3), 345–361.

Hackitt, J. (2017). Building a Safer Future—Independent Review of Building Regulations and Fire Safety (Trans: Government CaL). London.

HMICFRS. (2017). Proposed Fire and Rescue Services Inspection Programme and Framework 2018/2019. For Consultation. Her Majesty's Inspectorate of Constabulary and Fire and Rescue Services, London.

Home Office. (2017). Policing and Crime Act 2017. c.3.

Hood, C. (2010). Accountability and Transparency: Siamese Twins, Matching Parts, Awkward Couple? *West European Politics, 33*(5), 989–1009.

House of Commons Communities and Local Government Committee. (2011). *Select Committee: Audit and Inspection of Local Authorities—Fourth Report of Session 2010–12.* London.

House of Commons Public Accounts Committee. (2016a). *Financial Sustainability of Fire and Rescue Services Twenty-Third Report of Session 2015–16.* London.

House of Commons Public Accounts Committee. (2016b). *Managing Government Spending and Performance: Twenty-Seventh Report of Session 2016–17.* London: House of Commons.

Jones, M. (2017). English Resilience in the Face of Austerity. In I. Steccolini, M. Jones, I. Saliterer, & E. Berman (Eds.), *Governmental Financial Resilience: International Perspectives on How Local Governments Face Austerity* (pp. 73–91). Bingley: Emerald Publishing.

Knight, K. (2013). *Facing the Future: Findings from the Review of Efficiencies and Operations in Fire and Rescue Authorities in England.* London: Department of Communities and Local Government.

Lewis, B. (2017). *Fire Minister's Speech to Reform.* London: Home Office.

LGA. (2011a). *Taking the Lead: Self-Regulation and Improvement in Local Government.* London: Local Government Association.

LGA. (2011b). *What Is Sector-Led Improvement?* London.

LGA. (2014). *AnyFire: The Future Funding Outlook for Fire and Rescue Authorities.* London.

Lowndes, V., & McCaughie, K. (2013). Weathering the Perfect Storm? Austerity and Institutional Resilience in Local Government. *Policy & Politics, 41*(4), 533–549.

Lowndes, V., & Pratchett, L. (2012). Local Governance Under the Coalition Government: Austerity, Localism and the 'Big Society'. *Local Government Studies, 38*(1), 21–40.

May, T. (2016). *Home Secretary Speech on Fire Reform.* London: Home Office.

Ministry of Housing CLG. (2011). *Fire Futures Report: Government Response.* TSO. Retrieved March 17, 2018, from https://www.gov.uk/government/publications/fire-futures-report-government-response–2.

Murphy, P. (2015a). *Briefing Note on 'Financial Sustainability of Fire and Rescue Services-Value for Money Report' for the National Audit Office.* London: NAO.

Murphy, P. (2015b). *Flood Response Hit by Regional Austerity Cuts. The Conversation.* Retrieved March 22, 2018, from http://theconversation.com/flood-response-hit-by-regional-austerity-cuts-23448.

Murphy, P., Glennon, R., Lakoma, K., & Spencer, T. (2018). *Response to the Proposed Fire and Rescue Service Inspection Programme and Framework 2018/2019: Her Majesty's Inspectorate of Constabulary and Fire & Rescue Services Consultation.* Nottingham: Nottingham Trent University.

Murphy, P., & Greenhalgh, K. (2011a). Strategic Review Offers Unique Opportunity. *Fire,* January, London.

Murphy, P., & Greenhalgh, K. (2011b). *Final Report of the Independent Appraisal of Data Collection, Systems and Modelling for the Fire Cover Review.* Nottingham: Nottingham Trent University.

Murphy, P., & Greenhalgh, K. (2014). *Peer Challenge Needs an Independent Fire Inspectorate. Fire,* July/August, London.

Murphy, P., & Greenhalgh, K. (2018). *Fire and Rescue Services: Leadership and Management Perspectives.* Berlin: Springer.

NAO. (2015a). *Department for Communities and Local Government: Financial Sustainability of Fire and Rescue Services.* London: NAO.

NAO. (2015b). *Local Government Variation in Spending by Fire and Rescue Authorities 2011–2012 to 2013–2014.* London: NAO.

Neill, B. (2010). *Leading a Lean and Efficient Fire and Rescue Service.* London: Department for Communities and Local Government.

Pickles, E. (2010a). *Eric Pickles to Disband Audit Commission in New Era of Town Hall Transparency.* London: Department for Communities and Local Government.

Pickles, E. (2010b). *Local Government Accountability.* London: Ministry of Housing, Communities and Local Government.

Raynsford, N. (2016). *Substance Not Spin: An Insider's View of Success and Failure in Government.* Bristol: Policy Press.

The Guardian. (2012). Bonfire of the Quangos: The Victims. *The Guardian.* Retrieved August 22, 2012, from http://www.theguardian.com/politics/2012/aug/22/bonfire-quangos-victims-list.

Walker, A. (2015). *Resilience in Practice.* London: Local Government Information Unit.

Wankhade, P., & Murphy, P. (2012). Bridging the Theory and Practice Gap in Emergency Services Research: A Case for a New Journal. *International Journal of Emergency Services, 1*(1), 4–9.

CHAPTER 7

Public Service Accountability—Some Reflections

Peter Murphy, Russ Glennon and Laurence Ferry

Abstract This chapter provides a reflective examination across the four empirical chapters, and more generally across public services. It then goes on to generate ideas and avenues for future research. We argue that no single type or approach to accountability is 'best' and it is the multiple and contingent nature of accountability that requires consideration of the four different modes we explore in chapter two. We have, however, elevated accountability up into the position of superordinate concept over this field of concepts. We regret the loss of the key role previously played by the Audit Commission in this debate and hope to stimulate a richer and more complex debate on the nature of *public service account-ability*, including a clear focus on inductively developing and co-producing this hand-in-hand with practitioners.

Keywords Public service accountability · Conceptualisation Evaluation · Dialogic accountability

INTRODUCTION

The previous chapters have explored the conceptual foundations of accountability, established our evaluative model, and explored changes and reforms that have affected or influenced accountability within four key public service institutions: local government, health and social care, the police, and the fire and rescue services. Throughout the four

© The Author(s) 2019
P. Murphy et al., *Public Service Accountability*,
https://doi.org/10.1007/978-3-319-93384-9_7

empirical chapters, we have also used the evaluative model as a lens through which we could explore these changes. This chapter now moves on to provide a reflective examination across the four public services, and more generally, and then goes on to generate ideas and avenues for future research.

As stated in chapters one and two, this book does not seek to establish a normative model for how accountability should be implemented. Rather, we set out to contribute to the debate on accountability through examining some of the changes that have occurred, and exploring how accountability's broad conceptual footprint draws on a range of ideas, values, and practices and what that might mean for the notion of *public service accountability*.

The book took as a starting point some work commissioned by the National Audit Office (NAO) around public assurance. This sought to better understand what confidence the public (and politicians) might have in how well those public services were 'saying what they were doing and doing what they had said'. Whilst this addresses core elements of democratic accountability, we would contend that democracy as an accountability tool is necessary, but insufficient. Thus, we sought to tighten the focus for public services in such a way that allowed a more granular and nuanced perspective on accountability, which rebalances the significance of accountability as a *mechanism* and as a *virtue* (Bovens et al. 2014). Whether or how well we have done that is not for us to say—you will undoubtedly have your own views on that.

One important part of the context of these investigations, however, was the running down and closure of the Audit Commission by the Conservative-led coalition government. A recurring theme of the empirical chapters, and one that we discuss in chapters one and two, is that of transparency and its relationship with accountability (Hood 2010; Ferry et al. 2015; Ferry and Eckersley 2015; Ferry and Murphy 2018). This book argues that accountability operates as the overarching concept and that the framework of related concepts are best 'nested' within it. The external inspection and assurance provided by the Audit Commission was a fundamental component of UK, and more specifically English, public service accountability (Scotland and Wales now have alternative arrangements). The Audit Commission's inspection processes, and the regulatory frameworks to which the inspections were tied, explicitly bound together judgements on historical financial and performance achievement, as well as making explicit judgements on the future capacity and capability for improvement in the same areas. Whilst not the main subject of the book, the view that emerges from the empirical work, and from our considerations of wider accountability practices, is that the removal of the Audit Commission has diminished the quality of public service delivery. Whilst there were plenty of reasons to criticise the regulatory frameworks and the way they were implemented (Leach 2010; McLean et al. 2007) and, anecdotally at least, many practitioners echoed these criticisms (Glennon et al. 2018; Glennon 2017), the deregulation of performance, coupled with the dilution of professional auditing regimes, clearly makes holding public services to account more difficult, and their overall performance more opaque (Ferry et al. 2017; Ferry and Murphy 2015).

This is why our evaluative model draws upon and develops a more holistic and systemic perspective for *public service accountability*, and we suggest that this debate needs to be rekindled in public services.

Reading Across the Sectors

When we reflect on the lessons from across the four sectors, we observe patterns, commonalities, and differences between them; this is as it should be. We have argued that no single type or approach of accountability is 'best'. Instead, we suggest that it is the multiple and contingent nature of accountability that means that a consideration of the four different modes we explore in chapter two is necessary to develop and embed accountability practices more effectively in the four service institutions.

Local Government

Local government represents the most diverse of the four public services in terms of both the types of public services delivered and the range of accountability mechanisms put into practice. Local government should, therefore, be one of the most directly accountable institutional types. To some extent this is true, and because of this, local government (with fire and rescue services) is perhaps the area that has suffered most from the removal of the Audit Commission. External inspection still operates in some service areas, notably education and social services, but an accountability deficit has been created by the loss of systemic regulation of performance, finance, planning, and strategic management generated by council-wide accountability regimes such as CPA and CAA.

Austerity, a key feature in all four sets of investigations, has had a significant effect on service delivery, the full extent of which is perhaps only now becoming apparent. Attempts to increase transparency through 'armchair' auditing has not delivered on its promises; we argue this was never likely to happen and that the NAO is beginning to raise concerns about the clarity and transparency of local government service delivery.

Weakening of both prospective and retrospective forms of accountability and reliance on inadequate replacements such as transparency initiatives places central government in a position of being significantly less able to understand whether local government is delivering national policy objectives. It similarly makes local government less able to have a constructive dialogue with communities and between officers and members about how to manage services, for which we can read 'service reductions', within the climate of significant budgetary cuts.

Health and Social Care

The health and social care sector underwent considerable organisational and structural changes during 2010–2015, as well as experiencing a hostile public and political environment and significant challenges driven by demand levels and funding. Attempts to introduce transparency as a support for accountability have proven to be inadequate: see Hood's (2010) characterisation of accountability and transparency as an *awkward couple*. Unfortunately, this relationship had previously been stronger in practice, and accountability as a *virtue* (Bovens et al. 2014) had long been considered a fundamental feature of the sector—Bevan's 'dropped bedpan reverberating'. Changes inspired by New Public Management began a long, slow process of fragmenting the mechanisms of accountability, and this was accelerated by the *Health and Social Care Act 2012* and the *Local Audit and Accountability Act 2014*. However, some of the concerns generated by the creation of NHS England (i.e. the breaking of formal accountability on the part of the secretary of state) have fortunately not materialised. Nevertheless, it is clear that financial and service performance have become opaque, and that high-profile systemic failures such as the Mid Staffs scandal have allowed the NHS to continue as something of a 'political football'. Changes to accountability mechanisms may have been used to pin down blame rather than for genuine performance innovation and improvement.

Financial sustainability has risen to the top of the list of concerns for the NAO. Here, however, we find that prospective accountability remains challenging for the sector. There may be good reasons for this in parts; the NHS is a strongly demand-led service, but so too are most of the other services, particularly police and fire and rescue. Here, though, we have observed the impact of structural changes that place new organisations and governance structures into pre-existing lines of accountability. The end result is, unsurprisingly, disruption, and added complexity to accountability mechanisms. This has also happened in housing and local government and we are seeing moves to implement new forms of more political governance in the police and fire through 'blue light integration'. If we examine the history of such reforms, a healthy scepticism emerges as to whether such changes will strengthen or diminish accountability.

Police Services

The police services have experienced a slightly different trajectory to local government and health and social care, although there are still similarities. Whilst local government has seen a reduction in external inspection, the police force has seen a strengthening of external scrutiny through changes to the inspectorate—Her Majesty's Inspectorate of Constabulary (HMIC), and more recently Her Majesty's Inspectorate of Constabulary and Fire and Rescue Services (HMICFRS)—and the replacement of the Police Complaints Authority by the Independent Police Complaints Commission, and most recently the Independent Office for Police Conduct in 2017. Whilst it is too early to say whether this latter change will make significant improvements, the stiffening of external inspection is to be welcomed, particularly given that some police forces have recently been exposed to significant public, political, and media criticism around high-profile incidents, e.g. the Hillsborough Inquiry, historic sexual abuse complaints, and claims of institutional racism from the MacPherson report onwards. Additionally, the creation of police and crime commissioners (PCCs) as political interfaces that have replaced police authorities has also changed the landscape of policing. Whilst PCC elections have been democratically weak in terms of turnout (Lister and Rowe 2015), police authorities were not necessarily much stronger in this regard. PCCs have therefore continued an established trajectory of concentrating power in a few elected representatives, as can also be observed with city mayors.

These reforms appear to have given stronger political and managerial leadership to forces, and transparent and effective inspection criteria can provide a clear framework for prospective accountability. However, the impact of austerity appears to be challenging the ability of the police to effectively resource and deliver prevention and protection services, especially given recent terrorist attacks. Here, too, the NAO is raising questions around financial sustainability and the police's ability to be transparent about resourcing priorities and future service delivery, which may have been affected.

Fire and Rescue Services

Finally, we come to fire and rescue services, which have also been following a different, if still familiar, path. A series of significant and public events, including terrorist incidents and the Bradford and King's Cross fires, had been influential in changes in the roles, responsibilities, and operational practices of the fire and rescue services. These resulted in changes in legislation, with the *Fire and Rescue Services* and *Civil Contingencies Acts in 2004* and these were translated into successive national fire frameworks. Since 2010, however, the Audit Commission's external inspection and performance assessment has been superseded by the rise in prominence of peer inspection and sector-led improvement. This has had the effect of driving accountability down towards the local level, rather than national level, as well as localising the focus on value for money. This has been the subject of considerable criticism, and the NAO focus here was on the need for financial sustainability and a new independent inspectorate.

During this time, fire and rescue services retained their governance and scrutiny body, the fire authority. However, the creation of PCCs has influenced thinking around fire and rescue governance and scrutiny. This was coupled with challenges in collecting and analysing performance information caused by several factors: insufficient control of national data collection, financial austerity, and the *Knight Review* in 2013. The reform trajectory for fire and rescue clearly points towards greater integration with police structures, also known as 'blue light integration'. We do not have sufficient space here to critique this development, but at the time of writing a small number of fire and rescue services are proposing police, fire and crime commissioners (PCFCs) to facilitate integration at the governance level, although none have felt it appropriate to propose operational integration. Nonetheless, the presumption from central government is to move towards integration and a more direct politicisation of governance and scrutiny than has been afforded by the previous councillor-led fire authority model.

As with police forces, these reforms have had some positive effects on accountability through increased clarity of leadership and objective-setting. This would seem to have aided some of the prospective mechanisms for accountability, and the recent consultation and piloting of the new fire framework also suggests this is becoming clearer. However, this is still offset by insufficient data collection and analysis, and the new framework itself is not yet able to resolve the problems caused by variations in data being collected at the local service level. The NAO has raised concerns about financial sustainability and the capturing of inter-agency efficiencies.

Evaluating Public Service Accountability

Our goal in this book was threefold: to develop an understanding of the status quo of accountability in locally delivered public services, to draw some lessons from across those services, and to propose an approach that might help practitioners and academics in working to enhance the quality and value for money of public service delivery.

The earlier work for the NAO, from which the empirical portions of this book derive, articulated a situation where a range of reforms implemented by central government have created challenges by obscuring whether or how much these four services are delivering what is needed, to the level desired by the public, and in a sustainable way. We are not necessarily suggesting that none of the institutions within the four areas are delivering effective services—we are acutely aware of the dedication, effort, and intellect brought to bear by committed public servants. Rather, we argue that it is extremely difficult for them to be able to demonstrate this using the current frameworks and regulatory environment.

Thus, the original work for the NAO considered ten concepts and focused more closely on two: accountability and transparency. Here, we attempt to move this work forward by embracing a wider conceptual horizon for accountability, which we return to as the overarching concept. We also attempt to frame the debate by using our evaluative model proposed in this book, which we hope will support a more evidence-based debate around what the most appropriate forms of accountability mechanisms may be.

Drawing from across our work we have highlighted three key elements for the development of effective accountability:

- Balancing forward-looking and backward-looking forms
- Negotiating the tensions between centrally imposed and locally determined accountabilities (and individual and systemic) forms
- The integration of financial and performance accountability along with quantitative and qualitative methods to promote a dialogue of accountability.

We have also tried to avoid making value judgements at the individual service level. However, we have drawn out some commonalities across the four service types. Foremost amongst these are:

- The impact of austerity
- The deregulation of performance frameworks, leading to lack of formal information analysis capability
- An overreliance on transparency and amateur arrangements—these are palpably not working
- Real difficulties in understanding and expressing value for money, in part owing to the three commonalities above. The conception of what value for money is within public services probably needs to change.

Underpinning this is our view that traditional principal/agent understandings of accountability are limited and problematic. We highlight two key issues: the multiple agent, multiple principals problem, and the difficulties of dyadic relationships. We have also suggested, as have others, that whilst democratic accountability is, and should continue to be, a fundamental aspect of accountability, this largely speaks to the concept of accountability as a *virtue* (Bovens et al. 2014), and that effective accountability requires strong mechanisms.

The principal/agent approach lends itself too easily to a combative, sanctions-based view of how accountability should operate. We prefer to move beyond merely 'answerability' and argue that accountability should be considered as a conversation or dialogue between the multiple stake-holders, and not just between central government and local agencies, and thence between agencies and the users of their services. This should be based around an honest appraisal of what resources are available, what needs are present, and how the two are best aligned.

Embracing the notion of a more 'dialogic accountability' should address our three key elements, and we hope to make a contribution to the wider realms of accountability practice. We will now provide our final conclusions and some recommendations, as well as some avenues for future research.

OVERALL CONCLUSIONS AND RECOMMENDATIONS

We have suggested that the multiple and contingent nature of account-ability is one of the features that has repeatedly confounded reforms in *public service accountability*. The mechanisms, and indeed some of the aspects of the virtue, of accountability are contingent on the context of the service. Local government highly values democratic representation and the primacy of the political process. This is becoming more visible in police forces and fire and rescue service through the development of PCC and now PFCC roles. Yet local government has a wider range of community-relationship and engagement activities and roles than the other two, and certainly more than health and social care, which has not seen the same sorts of political interface develop at the very local level. We are strong advocates for democratic engagement and accountability, but how this will operate in practice for the emergency services is still unclear. The ethos and values behind police and fire and rescue are very different, and the public engages with them in very different ways. This is not to say that services cannot learn from each other—they assuredly can—but the approaches to establishing the most suitable accountability arrangements across the four modes we have outlined requires a greater granularity of context-specific analysis.

On the other hand, we have also noted that the accountability chal-lenge is getting more complex and more diverse, and services should be learning more from each other more than is happening. This has, in part, been impeded by a lack of formal public performance and finan-cial information. Similarly, the pace and locus of reforms is demonstrably different in the four areas we consider. Fire and rescue, for example, is in the early stages of implementing a new inspection and performance framework—an experience the police force has recently been through but one that local government is moving away from. Consistent and robust performance and financial management, or the lack thereof, is clearly causing difficulties in establishing a clear baseline of delivery.

This leads us to conclude that it is becoming extremely challenging for public services to secure continuous improvement in terms of financial performance (i.e. due to austerity) or service performance (because of austerity again, but also the deregulation of performance). This is a problem for local government in particular, which is still under a duty to achieve *Best Value*, i.e. securing continuous improvement in its services with regard to the 3 Es, something recently confirmed in updated guidance (DCLG 2015).

Austerity has also stimulated a number of unintended (or perhaps not) consequences with regard to organisational structures and purposes. Health and social care saw the fragmentation of accountability as a result of the *Health and Social Care Act 2012*. New governance structures in police forces, and now fire and rescue services, are raising questions of amalgamation, back-office sharing, and inter-organisational efficiencies which have been a pressure on local government for many years. Here too, budgetary pressures appear to have facilitated service failure, leading to calls for further local government reorganisation and further structural reform.

We contend that these organisational and governance structures are a key context in which accountability operates, and are at least as important as establishing a level of overall democratic accountability.

Finally, the impact of 'losing' the Audit Commission as the primary body through which, in our view, *local public service accountability* was embedded and operated has been felt throughout the four sectors. Our conclusion here is that the Audit Commission was clearly in need of reform and reorganisation, but that abolishing it was not the answer; the problems this has caused are manifest. To use a popular saying, the baby has clearly been thrown out with the bathwater. The NAO has stepped into that space and, within their scope and resources, has performed admirably, making inroads by commissioning reports on the state of play, and issuing specific criticisms and concerns, but it cannot realistically replicate the depth of data gathering and analysis that the commission was able to deploy, even if it had the same strength of regulatory frameworks to provide tools for assessing performance and hence accountability. We would suggest that the NAO needs significant additional and complementary capacity, perhaps through a partner organisation or some other way of generating additional capacity. Whether these deficits are addressed remains to be seen.

Accountability as a Superordinate Concept?

We have pushed accountability up into the position of a superordinate concept over what is a broad terrain. The concepts we articulate in chapter one should nest underneath accountability, and be seen as part of the jigsaw puzzle. If we view public assurance as meaning 'say what you do and do what you say', then disappointingly we conclude that the capacity and capability to do so has significantly diminished.

A common interpretation of transparency is to shine a light on democracy. The last eight years or so have seen the window become more opaque, and the light filtered through the lens of increasingly politicised public services. Our ability to collect and analyse performance data has deteriorated, and even where this is being theoretically strengthened (i.e. with the development of a new fire framework), the current levels of variation in data collected means that establishing baselines and comparative analysis is extremely challenging. Deregulation of performance frameworks is at least partially to blame.

Scrutiny, governance, and systemic leadership have all become more challenging, and opinions are divided as to whether political commissioners are likely to improve this situation. Our experience suggests that very much depends on the quality of the commissioner, the regulatory framework and the service itself; time will tell.

It is, therefore, important to consider a more holistic model/whole system approach for accountability. This should cover financial sustainability and service performance to assess value for money in local public services (whether delivered by the public, private, or voluntary sectors), but also take account of the political, historical, and geographical contexts of governance and culture.

So, we conclude that accountability is a politically contested and complex landscape, both in theory and practice. Recent reforms have attacked any continuity in that landscape, which is, in any case, constantly evolving rather than static. It would appear that in England we are not keeping pace with changes in the challenge of ensuring that public services are held accountable for delivering what is needed, to the extent needed, and in a sustainable way.

Future Research Propositions

Finally, we suggest that this is a re-awakening of a necessary debate, and not solely a backward-looking reflection on the difficulties and mistakes of the last decade or so. We hope to stimulate a richer and more complex debate on the nature of *public service accountability*, including a clear focus on inductively developing and co-producing this hand-in-hand with practitioners. Our preference is for this to model the dialogic accountability conversation we are suggesting services should be having with their stakeholders. After all, we are all stakeholders in the delivery of excellent public services—whether those be universal services or those targeting the most vulnerable in society. We do not profess to have the answers to the dilemmas, but rather we hope we have raised some of the right questions.

To this end, we conclude this book with a small number of research propositions drawn from across our narrative. We hope that these stimulate further research and debate.

- Can we use the four modes of accountability to establish working profiles for public services that reflect the contingent demands on each service?
- What are the most appropriate governance mechanisms in place to provide leadership, management and, crucially, internal scrutiny and oversight?
- What is the relationship between culture and accountability?
- How do we balance central direction and local discretion in terms of how services are configured and what they must deliver?
- How can we measure the value added by approaches that focus on co-creation of value between publics and public services?
- What role should external regulation or inspection play? What additional resource, process, or expertise is needed to cover gaps in understanding financial and performance accountability?
- How can divergent forms of dialogic accountability processes need to be conceived and supported?

Finally, we, as residents, citizens, service users, customers, taxpayers, or clients, have the right to expect strong public services that address the needs we have. How can the government best assure us that this is being achieved?

We may have only scratched the surface here of a much larger and important debate. We encourage everyone to get involved in the governance and scrutiny of our public services. Whilst, we may be sceptical about the ability of armchair auditors or amateur performance analysts, we believe passionately in the need and responsibility of us all as citizens to engage beyond the ballot box alone and participate in that dialogue with public services. Good luck.

References

Bovens, M., Schillemans, T., & Goodin, R. E. (2014). Public Accountability. In M. Bovens, R. E. Goodin, & T. Schillemans (Eds.), *The Oxford Handbook of Public Accountability* (pp. 1–22). Oxford: Oxford University Press.

DCLG. (2015). *Revised Best Value Statutory Guidance*. London: TSO.

Ferry, L., & Eckersley, P. (2015). Accountability and Transparency: A Nuanced Response to Etzioni. *Public Administration Review, 75*(1), 11–12.

Ferry, L., Eckersley, P., & Zakaria, Z. (2015). Accountability and Transparency in English Local Government: Moving From 'Matching Parts' to 'Awkward Couple'? *Financial Accountability & Management, 31*(3), 345–361.

Ferry, L., Gebreiter, F., & Murphy, P. (2017). Written Evidence Submitted to the Public Accounts Committee on Financial Sustainability of the NHS. Public Accounts Committee.

Ferry, L., & Murphy, P. (2015). *Financial Sustainability, Accountability and Transparency Across Local Public Service Bodies in England Under Austerity* (Report to National Audit Office (NAO)). London: National Audit Office.

Ferry, L., & Murphy, P. (2018). What About Financial Sustainability of Local Government!—A Critical Review of Accountability, Transparency, and Public Assurance Arrangements in England During Austerity. *International Journal of Public Administration, 41*(8), 619–629.

Glennon, R. (2017). *The 'Death of Improvement': An Exploration of the Legacy of Performance and Service Improvement Reform in English Local Authorities, 1997–2017*. Loughborough: Loughborough University.

Glennon, R., Hodgkinson, I. R., Knowles, J., Radnor, Z., & Bateman, N. (2018). The Aftermath of Modernisation: Examining the Impact of a Change Agenda on Local Government Employees in the UK. *Australian Journal of Public Administration* (Forthcoming).

Hood, C. (2010). Accountability and Transparency: Siamese Twins, Matching Parts, Awkward Couple? *West European Politics, 33*(5), 989–1009.

Leach, S. (2010). The Audit Commission's View of Politics: A Critical Evaluation of the CPA Process. *Local Government Studies, 36*(3), 445–461.

Lister, S., & Rowe, M. (2015). Electing Police and Crime Commissioners in England and Wales: Prospecting for the Democratisation of Policing. *Policing and Society, 25*(4), 358–377.

McLean, I., Haubrich, D., & Gutiérrez-Romero, R. (2007). The Perils and Pitfalls of Performance Measurement: The CPA Regime for Local Authorities in England. *Public Money and Management, 27*(2), 111–118.

INDEX

© The Editor(s) (if applicable) and The Author(s) 2019
P. Murphy et al., *Public Service Accountability*,
https://doi.org/10.1007/978-3-319-93384-9

Printed by Printforce, the Netherlands